W9-BNA-632

WHAT WOULD FRIDA DO?

WHAT WOULD FRIDA DO?

A Guide to Living Boldly

ARIANNA DAVIS

SEAL PRESS
NEW YORK

Cover design by Chin-Yee Lai
Cover illustration by Kimberly Glyder

Seal Press
Hachette Book Group
1290 Avenue of the Americas, New York, NY 10104
www.sealpress.com
@sealpress

Printed in the United States of America

First Edition: October 2020

Published by Seal Press, an imprint of Perseus Books, LLC, a subsidiary of Hachette Book Group, Inc. The Seal Press name and logo is a trademark of the Hachette Book Group.

The Hachette Speakers Bureau provides a wide range of authors for speaking events. To find out more, go to www.hachettespeakersbureau.com or call (866) 376-6591.

The publisher is not responsible for websites (or their content) that are not owned by the publisher.

Interior art: Kimberly Glyder

Print book interior design by Chin-Yee Lai

Library of Congress Control Number: 2020943711

ISBNs: 978-1-5416-4632-2 (hardcover), 978-1-5416-4631-5 (ebook)

LSC-C

Printing 5, 2021

To

FRIDA KAHLO,

who has taught me
the most important lesson of all:
"Viva la vida!"

CONTENTS

WHAT WOULD FRIDA DO?

INTRODUCTION

The streets of Mexico City's southern neighborhood Coyoacán are quiet. Colorful houses with intricate iron gates dot avenues named after cities in Europe: Paris, Berlin, Madrid. Suddenly, on Calle Londres, the stillness is broken. Dozens of people are buzzing about, some standing on their toes to get a glimpse at the front of a line that wraps around the block. From 1907 through 1954, this electric-blue house was home to Frida Kahlo.

Since 1958, "La Casa Azul" has been known as Museo Frida Kahlo, or the Frida Kahlo Museum, a donation from the artist's husband, Diego Rivera, who wanted the home he shared with his wife to become a tribute to her work. And more than six decades after her death, the house still feels full of life.

When I first walk through the tall green entryway beneath the words "Museo Frida Kahlo," I'm greeted by a large patio surrounded by walls so vibrantly blue they almost hurt the eyes; a jungle-like assortment of greenery and cacti hugs the trunks of palm trees that stretch toward the sky. Before heading inside, I spot a small stone bench off to the side and sit down to drink it all in. I close my eyes to focus on the sound of water sprinkling from a fountain; the autumn air is crisp and cool, and the scent of earth and moss clings to my skin. Overhead, leaves sway and birds caw cheerfully. And then, when I open my eyes, she's there: a young Frida Kahlo limping through the garden, her skirt sweeping the floor as she hums "Cielito Lindo" to herself. Her hairless dog, Señor Xolotl, scurries behind her. When the front door swings open, she turns, a radiant smile spreading across her face. "Diego!" she cries. I smile, too.

And then, as quickly as it began, my daydream is interrupted by a squeal. A tall, lanky blonde is yelling "Excuse me!" as she trips over my foot. Apparently, I'm in the way; she's been angling into this spot for a photo. After I shimmy to the side, she strikes the perfect influencer pose as her friend snaps away on her iPhone. As soon as they leave, I sigh with relief that I can return to my peaceful revelry with Frida—but no sooner does the blonde leave than a gaggle of high school girls in matching Frida Kahlo tees arrive, chatting in Japanese as they snap selfies. Behind them, it seems the crowd that has been let into the *museo* has nearly doubled in size; a chorus of accents fills the previously peaceful space as visitors jostle one another to try to enter the home.

Outside the museum, every corner of Frida's beloved neighborhood—the place where she was born and where she died, where she fell in love with her husband, where she painted some of her most moving works, and where she always returned after every stint living abroad—is crowded with

Frida graffiti, posters, and souvenir carts. For several blocks, you can find a woman on every corner wearing a Frida-style costume calling out that she has items for sale from a basket full of T-shirts, wallets, and tiny twee dolls with felt unibrows. Keep walking toward the center of town, and the stalls of street markets overflow with goods decorated with Frida's image, everything from dangling beaded earrings to cooking aprons, jewelry boxes, matchboxes, slip-on shoes, iPhone cases, and . . . salad bowls. And this level of Frida adulation extends far beyond the magical, art-filled streets of Coyoacán.

Since the 1990s, "Fridamania" has been in full swing around the world. The artist's posthumous popularity only increases every year, and at this point it's clear that Fridamania is not a passing trend; the world will forever be infatuated with her image, life, art, and legacy. Thanks to a resurgence of her work during the women's rights and Chicano movements in the 1980s, by the next decade, the late Frida had become a full-blown celebrity. A 2002 Oscar-winning biopic starring Salma Hayek only further fueled our culture's obsession with her. Now, her influence can be felt thousands of miles away from Mexico City, reaching as far as the museums of Europe, the kitschy shops of Tokyo, and . . . well, basically anywhere the internet can reach.

Give her name a quick google, and you will find Frida Kahlo keychains. Frida Kahlo wallets. Frida Kahlo magnets, mugs, and music boxes. Frida Kahlo socks, suitcases, and scents. Frida Kahlo beach bags, pens, tequilas, nail polishes, coffee machines, makeup palettes, credit cards, kimonos, sneakers, garden planters. There are even sanitary napkins. (Yes, you read that right.) Her face adorns the walls of chain restaurants and postcards that spin around merchandise carousels in college bookstores. Universities around the world hold entire courses about the artist's work. Chain retailers like Vans have released merchandise collections featuring her face. In 2017, to mark what would have been her 110th birthday, the Dallas Museum of Art held a "Frida Fest" where attendees set a Guinness World Record for the largest gathering of people dressed like Frida Kahlo. During the coronavirus pandemic quarantine in 2020, small online retailers like Artelexia in San Diego, California, quickly sold out of Frida Kahlo jigsaw puzzles.

Long before smartphones turned millions of people into aspiring influencers like the ones I bumped into at the museo, there was the artist who would empower generations of women to embrace their own images: Frida Kahlo. Of course, Frida was not the first person to paint a self-portrait; in fact, as far as historians know, the first panel-style self-portrait in history is 1433's *Portrait of a Man in a Turban*, by Jan van Eyck. But it *was* Frida Kahlo who uniquely transformed self-portraits into an art of storytelling for women, depicting the ins and outs of her life—both the love and the pain—in the same way millions of people today overshare on social media. It's just that now, instead of careful strokes of a paintbrush, we can simply capture quick snaps on a phone and upload them with just the right caption.

Fans of Frida Kahlo often discuss how the queer, disabled, and revolutionary artist would feel about the endless modern interpretations of her story. Would the admittedly self-centered artist bask in the adulation, or would she be horrified at the commodification of her image—at how watered-down her ideals, politics, and works have become? Some of these depictions have even stirred up controversy. In 2018, Mattel released a Frida Kahlo Barbie doll as part of its Inspiring Women line. The doll came complete with Frida's signature flower-braided hairstyle and Mexican-inspired dress, but it was missing a few key attributes, including her unibrow, or any of the medical devices she needed for her disabilities (various corsets through the years and, later in life, a prosthetic leg). The doll—which also inexplicably featured lightened eyes—drew criticism from Frida's family and estate, as well as from fans who believed that Frida would have hated nothing more than seeing herself as a commercialized doll with unrealistic bodily proportions and beauty features.

And now, here I am, sitting down to write a book on the life of Frida Kahlo, adding one more to the dozens of volumes about the artist that already line bookshelves around the world. Here's where I should clarify that this work is in no way meant to be an extensive biography, or to speak from Frida's perspective. Instead, this read will take a look at the various ways we can *all* glean lessons from Frida Kahlo's life—while learning a little bit more about it, too. By examining the influence Frida has continued to have on our culture after her death, I hope to share how the legacy of one of history's most iconic women can inspire anyone looking to live a little more boldly. Frida was, above all else, a master of self—the author of her own story. So it's possible that Frida Kahlo might have *loved* the idea of a book celebrating her as a proudly Mexican, rule-breaking feminist artist; she might have even been delighted by the title: *What Would Frida Do?*

But it's also very possible that Frida Kahlo might have detested the idea of this very book. She was an outspoken, anticapitalist woman of strong opinions and convictions, and she was not shy about making her feelings known.

Because of this realization, whenever I sit down in front of my laptop, I feel as though Frida Kahlo is watching my every keystroke. The moment I begin to type, it's as though she is sitting across from me, frowning in an oversized armchair while she smokes a cigarette. She is as present as she was to me that day in the patio of her home in Coyoacán—no ghost or phantom, but a person as real as myself. On some days, her hair is decorated with bright-white gardenias, and on others, she wears a crown of rich fuchsia bougainvillea. Dark-brown irises peer at me from beneath that famously connected pair of brows. And currently, they are furrowed.

The more I write, the more self-conscious I become about the prose that might elicit eye rolls from this fictional Frida. And before I know it, she speaks, a lilt accenting the syllables of her warm alto as she flicks ash from her cigarette. After squinting her eyes and staring at me for a few moments, she asks bluntly, "Are you Mexican?"

I should have seen this coming. Nervously, I blabber the explanation that while I'm not Mexican, I *am* half Puerto Rican and half Black—and very proud to be writing this book as both a Latina and a woman of color who has admired her work and life for years. In my imagination, she huffs before following up with a rant about how she doesn't know how I can *stand* to live in New York City—or "Gringolandia" as she calls it. With a sigh, I remind her that I *did* make my way to her home in Mexico City to research her story and paid careful attention to detail as I captured her identity, culture, and influences. She paces back and forth from the window . . . and after a few minutes:

"Well, if it is *you* writing this thing, don't just give me compliments!" she says. "I *hate* flattery! Tell the people whether I had any real *talent*!"

I wonder, briefly, whether I'm going crazy from too many late nights of writing furiously. Or whether it's at all possible this is the same Frida a docent told me is rumored to wander the rooms of the Museo Frida Kahlo in Mexico City. There, curators like to say that, sometimes, Frida returns to her old home after dark; her shape has been seen filling out corsets and skirts as if she's borrowing her old clothing for the night.

But of course, the apparition looking over my shoulder when I type is simply the Frida of my imagination—a mental rendering my mind has created after years of wandering her art exhibits, reading her biographies, googling her quotes, and watching Salma Hayek as *Frida* one too many times. In fact, it wasn't until I was a few months into working on this book that I was able to hear what Frida *actually* sounded like when she was alive. In May 2019, an audio recording was unearthed by the Fonoteca National, Mexico's national sound library. In it, a voice believed to be Frida's reads from an essay she wrote about her husband, Diego, in 1949. Of course, there's no way to verify for sure whether it's indeed Frida speaking; I personally was surprised to hear how feminine and delicate the voice was, a departure from the rough-and-tumble alto I had been expecting. But then again, Frida was—and still is, in my case—full of surprises.

Regardless of how, exactly, her voice sounded, by the time I type these words, I feel as though I've studied the artist thoroughly enough to have some sense of what she might say if she could speak to me now. (I won't bore you with too many more details of her visits, but know that there are many evenings when I feel her suddenly reading over my shoulder before walking away slowly, frowning in dissatisfaction as she looks out the window. The smell of cigarette smoke and Guerlain's Shalimar perfume often linger long after she's disappeared.)

So following my imagined Frida's advice, I don't ever confuse the task of writing a book about the *real* Frida Kahlo's life as an assignment to publish chapters full of only her goodness. In fact, from the beginning of her career, history's most famously self-centered artist was, ironically, averse to praise. When she first presented her artwork in 1928 to Diego Rivera—the famed Mexican muralist who would later become her husband—the then twenty-one-year-old told him, "I have not come to you looking for compliments. I want the criticism of a serious man. I'm neither an art lover nor an amateur. I'm simply a girl who must work for her living."

That simple girl who had to work for a living had no idea that someday in the far future—decades after her last breath—one of her paintings, *Two Lovers in a Forest*, would sell for $8.1 *million* in New York City, the highest price for a work by any Latin American artist, ever. But Frida likely wouldn't care about the splashy price tag. Rather, she would want to know: What did the people *say* about her painting?

Still, though the artist claimed to hate flattery, she was also the woman who painted 143 paintings in her lifetime—that we know of, anyway—with 55 of them being self-portraits. Like much of her life, this is yet another example of a contradiction: her insistence that she hated flattery directly contrasts with her constant celebration of herself. But, really, that shouldn't be at all surprising. Frida Kahlo was a woman of contradictions, one who loved her husband dearly while engaging in passionate extramarital affairs; one who painted her pain while insisting that she was strong; one who embraced femininity through intricate hairstyles and

Revlon lipsticks while also dabbling in wearing men's suits and enhancing her thick eyebrows and visible mustache.

It's after considering all these facts that I finally realize that *this* is the Frida we can—and should—take inspiration from: a woman who was only as perfect as her flaws. My fictional Frida claps slowly as she sees the realization hitting me. "Finally," she says, without even bothering to mask her exasperation. And then, after several moments and more than a few sighs, my imagined Frida sits back, shoots me a considered look, and tells me—with just the hint of a smile—that if I *am* going to write this book, I'd better include all of her best quotes. Even the curse words.

It's been more than six decades since Frida Kahlo died in 1954, and now, pop culture around the world exists in an era of superfandom. Members of the Beyhive buzz around Beyoncé. The Arianators gather their tween forces to support Ariana Grande. Lady Gaga has assembled an army with her take-us-as-we-are Monsters.

So it's not hard to imagine that if the artist Frida Kahlo had been born just a handful of decades later, she, too, might have had her own passionately devoted fan base. The Friducitas, we might be called. Or maybe the Frida Fans. Perhaps Los Fridos, as she used to call her art students. Or even better: the Friduchas, a play on her childhood nickname. Yes—that's the one.

Recently, as I walked down the hallway toward my New York studio apartment, juggling my purse and keys as I rifled through my mail, a neighbor waved to get my attention. In this city, neighborly chitchat does not exist—but on this particular day, the woman stopped in her tracks to gesture toward me and smile. "Hey!" she said cheerfully. "I love your shirt!" Confused, it took me a moment to look down and realize she was showing appreciation for the watercolor graphic of Frida Kahlo emblazoned across my chest, a T-shirt I'd purchased from an Etsy shop years ago. My suspicion quickly dissipated as I responded with a smile of my own, a show of love for my fellow Friducha. For the next several minutes, the two of us—complete strangers, save for our address—bonded over a shared love for the artist. Now, whenever we bump into each other, we often swap info about Frida exhibits or events we've heard about in the city.

We might not be as organized as the Monsters or as ready to report for social media battle as the Beyhive, but we Friduchas are here, carrying a torch that burns far brighter and wider than even she could have imagined as an artist who reached midlevel fame during her years painting in Mexico City.

We are the people carrying Frida Kahlo tote bags we picked up on a whim while vacationing in Mexico; the writers wearing watercolor Frida Kahlo T-shirts; the families spending Sunday afternoons in museum exhibits full of Frida Kahlo paintings; the couples touring La Casa Azul. We are the social media junkies who have contributed to nearly four million #FridaKahlo hashtags on Instagram, and who pin and share oft-repeated Frida Kahlo quotes. We are the slightly obnoxious dinner guests who drop fun Frida facts in the middle of conversation, both to make ourselves sound smarter and also because, well . . . *is* there any better solution to a lull in conversation than the storied life of Frida Kahlo?

Somehow, at one point or another, we've all fallen beneath Frida's spell, perhaps without even realizing it. Our enchantment might have been sparked by a memorable quote that inspired us to be our boldest, best selves, or through a viewing of the ethereal Julia Taymor–directed *Frida.* Possible, too, that we just fell down an internet rabbit hole one day while reading about her tempestuous marriage to fellow artist Diego Rivera. Or perhaps we became enamored with Frida thanks to the purest method: standing in front of a piece of her work and being transfixed not just by her ethereal brushstrokes and whimsical technique but also by those *eyes.* Warm, heartbroken, and somehow alive, as though her soul is piercing through both pain and time to let us know: she sees us.

It's not uncommon, obviously, for artists to only find great fame and appreciation after their death. Sometimes it takes the passage of time for a culture to fully realize the true impact of a human being. But how, exactly, did Frida manage to transform from a rising artist—one whose work was just beginning to emerge from behind her husband's shadow—into a household name who is celebrated around the world?

I first fell in love with the unibrowed Mexican artist when I was fifteen years old and saw the movie *Frida.* Of course, as a Latina, I was familiar with her status as an empowering icon, and I had learned briefly about her art in school. But it was watching Salma Hayek depict an artist whose passion and creativity flowed through everything from her paintbrush to her outfits to her love affairs that sparked what would become a lifelong fascination.

That obsession manifested itself in college research papers, dozens of books on my coffee table, afternoons spent wandering her exhibits, and an understanding among my loved ones that for me, Frida is a rock star. Christmas and birthday gifts over the years have included Frida Kahlo earrings, postcards, framed prints, and even a beach bag; to this day, I carry a beat-up wallet I once purchased in Mexico that features her pensive eyes. But over time, she's become much more than just a beautiful image; it's Frida's story that has made her a hero for me. The woman who survived accidents and a lifetime of debilitating pain—both physical and emotional—while still creating stunning works that our culture reveres to this day is now a legend to me. And it's the words she painted on one of her last paintings that solidified my appreciation for her: "Viva la vida!" or "Long live life!" For me, Frida the woman is a badass symbol of strength and courage—a real person who showed us by example that no matter what obstacles life throws our way, we all have the power to be the authors of our own stories.

Still, the life of this icon is shrouded in much uncertainty; her legacy leaves behind many rumors, misattributed quotes, and plenty of questions unanswered. No matter how much you know about her, there is still so much to learn. And most of us are hungry to know—who was Frida Kahlo *really?*

Frida Kahlo was born on July 6, 1907, as Magdalena Carmen Frieda Kahlo y Calderón. Her story began in a small house that would eventually become known as La Casa Azul in the village of Coyoacán, Mexico City. Her father, Guillermo Kahlo, was a painter from Germany who immigrated to Mexico; he and her mestiza mother, Matilde Calderón y González—of Spanish and indigenous Mexican descent—raised Frida and her three sisters, Matilde, Adriana, and Cristina. (Frida also had two half sisters from Guillermo's first marriage who were raised in a convent.)

From an early age, Frida learned that she had many odds against her. At age six she contracted polio, an infectious disease that weakens the muscles and sometimes stunts growth, leaving Frida with one leg shorter than the other for the rest of her life. And at eighteen, she was in a bus accident that would sentence her to a lifetime of endless operations, chronic pain, and the inability to bear children. And then there was the complicated relationship with her mother; Frida's mother constantly worried about her daughter's appearance, understanding that her physical challenges would affect her marrying prospects—and she wasn't quiet about it. In the 1999 book *Kahlo* by Andrea Kettenmann, Frida is quoted as having once said that her mother was "kind, active, and intelligent . . . but also calculating, cruel, and fanatically religious."

Frida didn't grow up wanting to be a painter. Her interest in art and, eventually, self-portraits didn't begin until age eighteen. In 1925, while riding the bus home from school with her boyfriend, Alejandro Gómez Arias (a classmate at the private National Preparatory School in Mexico City), a street trolley collided with the bus. Frida survived the accident, but barely, landing in the hospital with several spinal injuries, fractured ribs, a broken collarbone, and a shattered pelvis, the result of a handrail that pierced her body and exited through her vagina.

The healing process kept Frida bedridden in a full-body corset for over three months. The long road to recovery meant the end of her hopes to head to medical school, so instead—inspired by her extended hospital stay—she began to consider a career as a medical illustrator. Soon, using her father's oils, she was dabbling with painting, and her work slowly expanded from still lifes to portraits of friends and family. And then, when her parents brought in an easel and positioned it so that Frida could paint from bed, Frida began to spend endless hours looking in the mirror to discover the person who would become her favorite subject: herself.

If there was one thing Frida may have adored more than her own image and story, it was love. Throughout her lifetime, she would have more than a few torrid, passionate love affairs, her first being with Alejandro, to whom she wrote hundreds of angst-ridden letters while he traveled the world and grew increasingly distant from her after the accident.

But it was her marriage to Diego Rivera that was the most infamous. Frida got her first glimpse of the painter in 1922 when she was one of only thirty-five female students at the National Preparatory School. Diego was painting a mural in the auditorium. Rumor has it that Frida—the class mischief—used to play tricks on the painter, yelling out distractions at him as he painted. A few years later, the young girl Diego had previously encountered as a pesky prankster had grown into an aspiring painter who asked the famed muralist to review some of her work.

Although he never doubted her talent or her potential as an artist, Rivera quickly became more interested in reviewing . . . Frida. He "earnestly courted her" until they were married, when Frida was twenty-two years old and Diego was nearly twice her age, at forty-two. She was head over heels, and he was too, even though this was his third marriage and he was adamant about his inability to be monogamous. Before they wed, Frida's parents were apprehensive about the rumored womanizer—especially her mother, who called him the "elephant" to her "dove." But the pair embraced the monikers as loving nicknames that teased their physical differences.

Long before paparazzi would trail Elizabeth Taylor and Richard Burton or nickname Bennifer or Brangelina, Diego and Frida—each most commonly referred to by first name—were a glamorous couple whose exploits would often hit the papers as they crisscrossed the globe for various art projects and events. But several obstacles stood in the way of their happiness, including Frida's loneliness as her husband became increasingly tied up with his work—plus her never-ending surgeries and illnesses, which left her unable to bear children with Rivera.

And then there were the extramarital affairs. While it was no secret to Frida that her husband was a womanizer, the deeper the two fell into their marriage, the more hurtful his often public disloyalty became. Frida also dabbled in affairs, reportedly with both men and women, partaking in flings with everyone from Leon Trotsky to a rumored dalliance with dancer Josephine Baker. But despite infidelity on both of their parts, what truly shattered Frida and Diego's marriage was his extramarital affair with Frida's younger sister, Cristina.

The two divorced in 1939, a fraught period during which Frida continued to paint as her work began to gain recognition in art circles. But the duo quickly found their way back to one another later that same year, getting married for a second time on Diego's fifty-fourth birthday in 1940. The happiness of their reunion didn't last long, however; over the next decade, a lifetime of illness began to catch up to Frida, leading to her death from a pulmonary embolism in 1954 when she was forty-seven.

The dramatic story of Frida Kahlo's life is perhaps even better known than her work. But then again, with one look at her repertoire, you can see her entire tale, honest and uncensored—a stunning feat from any woman, but particularly from one who came of age during the 1920s and 1930s.

There's the 1932 piece called *Henry Ford Hospital* that she painted after a miscarriage, featuring herself hemorrhaging on a hospital bed. There's also the 1949 portrait *Diego and I*, painted after Frida discovered her husband's very public affair with film star Maria Felix. In it, Frida is without her signature braids or adornments, her hair wild and tangled around her neck; on a forehead wrinkled by worry lines is an image of a miniature Diego. And then, of course, there is *Thinking About Death*, a work that doesn't need much translation: Frida is long necked and bare, staring pensively straight ahead. The viewer gets another look inside her mind via a drawing on her forehead: a tiny skull and bones.

In other words? To know Frida Kahlo, you only need to study her artwork. There, her full story is laid bare: her surgeries and pain, her inability to carry children, her tumultuous marriage—and affairs—and her preoccupations with everything from sex to monkeys to death. But much of Frida's story is also now available in her own words, thanks to her journals and the hundreds of letters she wrote to friends, family members, doctors, and lovers. Much of this writing is what provides the quotes that now adorn Pinterest boards, refrigerator magnets, and posters in college dorm rooms—a lifetime of wisdom, anguish, and courage living on through trinkets and tchotchkes.

Decades later, Fridamania is in full effect—and not going anywhere. (Take a look at Google trends over the years, and you'll see that since 2004, searches about the artist have steadily increased, year by year.) But why *is* it that we are still so intrigued by Frida Kahlo? It's true that during her own lifetime she began to rise to notoriety, but she never came even close to being a household name the way she is now. In fact, it was sometime after her death that her artistry came to be recognized in its own right; for decades, she was known primarily as the quirky wife of Diego Rivera, one with a uniquely strange painting style.

In the 1970s, Frida began to slowly emerge as a feminist icon; she rose to fame thanks to Chicano artists who rediscovered her work and used her image as a symbol to represent Mexican women during marches and exhibitions. By the early eighties, her work was being featured in exhibitions around the world, as far away as Japan. And slowly but surely—with help from Hayden Herrera's 1983 biography and, later, that 2002 biopic—Frida's story, in addition to her artwork, became legendary.

Still, Frida Kahlo is far from the only famous woman with a tragic story who ever lived. Hilda Trujillo Soto, director of the Frida Kahlo Museum, has a theory as to what makes Frida stand out. "I think the world just keeps being interested in Frida because we keep getting little surprises from her, like in 2004, when we discovered more personal items from her house," Trujillo Soto tells me. She continues:

> *We knew she was a proud Mexican woman and wife to Diego, but then her belongings and letters showed us she was also a woman who loved jazz and French music—one*

> *who could speak English and German, one who didn't care about the rules for women. I think Frida would have loved the attention she's getting now. She would've been very proud to represent Mexican and Latina women and just women . . . and that she could teach people to be free.*

Frida Kahlo is a totemic symbol for hope, for change, for revolution, for resilience. There is no doubt that we can all learn endless lessons from the icon about how to live life loudly, boldly, and colorfully.

And so, my fellow Friduchas, here I go, diving in headfirst to explore the clues she left behind for those of us looking for guidance on how to emulate even just a little of her magic. With my imagined Frida looking over my shoulder, I embark on my search for the answer to a question many of us might want to ask ourselves during this journey we call life: *What would Frida do?*

THE RISE OF FRIDAMANIA

In 1933, a Detroit newspaper ran a story about Frida Kahlo with the headline "Wife of the Master Mural Painter Gleefully Dabbles in Works of Art." She had only two solo exhibitions of her work during her lifetime. So how, exactly, did Frida Kahlo progress from a woman in her husband's shadow to an icon?

1970S

The women's movement sparks renewed interest in Frida's life and work, and her image becomes a symbol for the feminist art and Chicano civil rights movements.

1978

Frida's 1944 painting *The Tree of Hope Stands Firm* is her first piece to be sold at auction, selling at Sotheby's for $19,000.

1982

A retrospective of Frida's art at the Whitechapel Gallery in London earns international attention, with the exhibition later traveling to Mexico, the United States, Sweden, and Germany. The rise of Neomexicanismo—a wave of art taking inspiration from Mexico's indigenous roots—also begins to shine another spotlight on Frida and her work.

1983

Art historian Hayden Herrera publishes an extensive biography of Frida Kahlo, *Frida: A Biography of Frida Kahlo*, which is translated into twenty-five languages and becomes the basis for a movie.

1985

Mexico City names a park in Coyoacán "Parque Frida Kahlo."

1990

Frida's portrait *Diego and I* auctions for nearly $1.5 million, making Frida the first Latina to sell a work for more than $1 million. The same year, singer Madonna purchases the paintings *My Birth* and *Self-Portrait*. She tells *Vanity Fair* that anyone who isn't a fan of *My Birth* can't be her friend.

2002

Salma Hayek stars in *Frida*, a biopic that wins two Academy Awards.

2004

After the passing of Dolores Olmedo, the friend who swore to Diego Rivera that she would keep the bathroom of La Casa Azul locked until fifteen years after his death, the room is opened, revealing Frida's personal letters, diaries, clothing, cosmetics, and even her prosthetic leg.

2006

Frida's 1943 painting *Roots* sells for $5.6 million at Sotheby's.

2010

To celebrate her 100th birthday (well, technically, her 103rd—Frida claimed she was born in 1910, with the Mexican Revolution, but was really born in 1907), Mexico releases a $500 bank note featuring Frida and Diego.

2016

Two Lovers in a Forest auctions for more than $8 million.

2018

Mattel releases a Frida Barbie—to much criticism over the doll's missing unibrow and slim waist.

2019

New York's Brooklyn Museum hosts *Frida Kahlo: Appearances Can Be Deceiving*, the largest Frida exhibition in the United States.

2020

London's English National Ballet livestreams *Broken Wings*, a ballet production inspired by Frida's life, free for fans to watch from home while quarantining during the coronavirus pandemic.

FRIDA KAHLO'S CELEBRITY FAN CLUB

As Frida Kahlo's legacy in the art world has grown after her death, so has her fan base—including plenty of celebrity Friduchas, like:

SALMA HAYEK

The Mexican actress worked tirelessly to produce the 2002 Academy Award–winning film *Frida*—and to portray Frida in it, beating out other big names in the running for the role, including Madonna and Jennifer Lopez. Today, she often posts odes to Frida on her Instagram, and she owns several of the artist's works.

MADONNA

Madonna has publicly shared her admiration for Frida, most recently by featuring a Frida portrait in her 2019 music video "God Control." The pop star has long been a vocal Frida fan, famously purchasing two of her most well-known paintings, *My Birth* and *Self-Portrait*, in the 1990s, and stating her desire to produce and star in a film about the artist. In 2015, the Detroit Institute of Arts held an exhibition titled *Diego Rivera and Frida Kahlo in Detroit*, showing works created by each of them. One piece was conspicuously missing: Frida's *My Birth*, which Madonna refused to loan to the museum.

COLDPLAY

In 2008, the British rock group Coldplay named their fourth album *Viva la Vida*, inspired by one of the last works Frida Kahlo painted. Frontman Chris Martin was adamant that people understand the real meaning had nothing to do with the 1999 pop song "Livin' La Vida Loca," by Ricky Martin, but was instead a tribute to Frida. He told *Rolling Stone*, "She went through a lot of shit, of course, and then she started a big painting in her house that said 'Viva la Vida.' . . . I just loved the boldness of it."

BEYONCÉ

In 2014, Beyoncé arrived at a Halloween party dressed as Frida Kahlo, donning a floral dress with a pussy bow, flower crown, and brushed-out brows. Art lovers also speculate that the imagery accompanying Bey's Instagram announcement that she was pregnant with twins might have been heavily influenced by Frida, given the tone, presence of flowers, and parallels between their stories as celebrities who had experienced challenges with infertility and their marriages.

THERESA MAY

In 2017, the then British prime minister infamously wore a bracelet decorated with Frida Kahlo's image during a speech to the Conservative Party, reportedly in an attempt to send the message that she cared about the marginalized . . . despite her widely known anti-immigration views.

ROSALÍA

In the artwork for her album *El Mal Querer*, the Spanish flamenco-pop singer re-created the iconic painting *Las dos Fridas*. In the original, two Fridas sit side by side, holding hands. In Rosalía's version, on one side she wears a white fur and veil, symbolizing purity and femininity, while on the other side she wears a black, male flamenco outfit, symbolizing darkness and masculinity. Fun fact: this album served as the soundtrack for much of the writing of this book; I like to think that, just as Rosalía is a fan of Frida, Frida would be a fan of the singer's unique style and her passion for transforming an old-school art form into a contemporary one.

1

CONFIDENCE

There are queens and movie stars and warriors and socialites. From Cleopatra to Beyoncé, when we look back through history, we find no shortage of women we can look to for inspiration on how to be confident. But there's also no doubt that Frida Kahlo's story makes her one of history's most inspiring female role models—a master at turning lemons into lemonade.

Combing through Frida's life to better understand how she went from a child prone to illness to one of the most well-known faces in history has been no easy task. It's required spending, essentially, my every waking moment with Frida. Before I knew it, she had taken over my life. Suddenly, during my daily travels through New York neighborhoods, I began to notice the subtle influences of Frida; she's there in the flick of a graffiti stroke, the sway of a passerby's skirt, the mariachi tunes floating out of a dimly lit bar. During conversations, I'd find words tumbling out of my mouth that sounded a lot like the ones Frida once wrote in her diary. Soon, her style had even seeped into my closet, the color palettes of my wardrobe becoming more vibrant, my accessory collection expanding to incorporate indigenous-inspired designs.

By the time I completed this book, I had begun to feel as though I might know Frida Kahlo better than anyone living in the entire world. But of course, the truth is that *actually* knowing Frida Kahlo is impossible. Even while she was alive, those around her only got to know a portion of Frida, the mask she chose to show the world via her paintings—and perhaps the same is true of her own husband, Diego. In fact, I believe that her biggest creative achievement wasn't her paintings at all, but instead the performance art that was her life—the drama she created with a main character who had such mystique and allure that generations have been carefully turning over her life in books and essays and exhibits and films ever since. Frida Kahlo was an enigma, a magician, a woman who reveled in being misunderstood.

There is, however, *one* thing we know for sure about Frida Kahlo: she was a badass, and she did not lack in confidence. As I study this woman who stood tall in her views—a feminist and communist who proudly rocked features that, still today, are often seen as anything but the typical standard of feminine beauty—I begin to contrast *that* Frida with the young woman who wore long skirts to conceal her crippled leg after being nicknamed "Peg Leg" by her peers. The comparison raises the question: was Frida truly confident . . . or was she just adept at hiding her insecurities?

Even someone with a minimal knowledge of art can take one look at Frida's portfolio and see *very* clearly that the

**I PAINT SELF-
PORTRAITS BECAUSE
I AM SO OFTEN ALONE,
BECAUSE I AM THE
PERSON I KNOW BEST.**

artist had no shortage of self-love—or narcissism, depending on how you look at it. And she was just as unapologetic in her real life as she was on canvas. Take, for instance, the words she penned to her husband, Diego Rivera, in one unsent letter: "I don't give a shit what the world thinks. I was born a bitch, I was born a painter, I was born fucked. But I was happy in my way. You did not understand what I am. I am love. I am pleasure, I am essence, I am an idiot, I am an alcoholic, I am tenacious. I am; simply I am."

"I am; simply I am." Those are the words of a woman who not only was comfortable in her own skin but actually *preferred* having flaws. It's important to remember that in her paintings and letters, Frida had the power to tell her own story her own way, as the creator of her own portraits and writer of her own narratives. But she never shied away from capturing the darkest details of her life, nor did she ever try to present herself as someone who was perfect or even likable. She was self-aware enough to admit that she was "born fucked" and "an alcoholic" while also being clear that she was her most loved subject. Her life offers a refreshing approach to finding confidence by simply *being*.

It's possible, of course, that Frida was born into the world with an extra set of armor to prepare her for all the pain that lay ahead of her. By all accounts, Frida was comfortable in her own skin starting in childhood—and though her relationship with her mother was, according to Frida herself, largely strained, Frida *did* have a close bond with her father, and he was the one who bolstered her from a young age. In her 1983 biography, *Frida*, author Hayden Herrera wrote that Frida described her relationship with her "Papa" as "marvelous . . . he was an immense example to me of tenderness, of work, and above all, in understanding for all my problems." It was Guillermo, also, who taught his daughter photography, one of her earliest lessons in creativity and self-expression.

And that self-expression quickly became . . . expressive, indeed. An early family portrait shows a seventeen-year-old Frida wearing a tweed men's pantsuit; her stance is cocky and defiant, as though she can already see the millions of people who will one day look at the photo and think, "A teenage girl in a men's suit in the 1920s? Bold!" It was also a move that was unlikely to have gone over well with her strict, religious mother—but it's clear that, by then, Frida Kahlo's favorite way to make a statement was through . . . Frida Kahlo.

Around this same time, Frida's father's printmaker friend Fernando Fernández began to give Frida drawing lessons, and her notebooks soon overflowed with sketches. There were no paintings, at least not yet. It wasn't until the bus accident in 1925, which sentenced her to many months in bed recuperating, that she began to experiment with painting. Using her father's paints and oils, she'd often create portraits of family, friends, and visitors—but her easiest subject was staring back at her from the mirror.

Over the next three decades, Frida would paint more than fifty-five portraits of herself. Her obsession with her own image may have started from those traumatic circumstances, and that is perhaps how it's possible that Frida could be at once so staunchly confident and so deeply insecure, a dichotomy that becomes obvious the more you look at her paintings.

Now, when we look back at Frida's work—especially as women—we can see the courage in her paintings. Hardly a selfie is posted to social media without a bit of editing, airbrushing, or nip-tucking, all possible thanks to a variety of apps available at our fingertips. Similarly, we can't forget that as the creator of her own image, Frida always had the option to paint herself in a different light—to remove her unibrow, lighten her skin, or soften her sharp features; in other words, to see herself through the lens of how society *thought* she should look, and then present that image for their acceptance. Instead? She represented herself exactly as she was. In every single brushstroke, Frida Kahlo celebrated herself.

Her adolescent confidence following her accident would also come in handy later, during Frida's adulthood, when she became the subject of newspaper articles and gossip, thanks to her high-profile marriage to Diego Rivera. Twenty years her senior when they wed in 1928, Diego was already an established, famous artist. His star continued to rise after they were married, and he was increasingly commissioned for lofty projects. For Frida, this meant being at her husband's side as he traveled from one hotly anticipated exhibition opening to another, everywhere from Europe to the United States—or as Frida so memorably put it, "Gringolandia."

In the beginning, during their newlywed phase, it seems from Frida's diaries, letters, and early interviews that she had no qualms about slipping into the role of the genius's wife, proudly standing by her husband's side. But soon it became apparent that Frida could not remain in his shadow for long. Take, for instance, an interview she did at age twenty-five with the *Detroit News* in 1932, when the couple was in town while Diego worked on several murals for the city.

When reporter Florence Davies asked Frida, "Are you a painter, too?" She quickly replied, "Yes. The greatest in the world." Later, Davies visited Frida at home for a profile that would be given the now incredibly ironic headline "Wife of

I AM LOVE.
I AM PLEASURE,
I AM ESSENCE,
I AM AN IDIOT,
I AM AN ALCOHOLIC,
I AM TENACIOUS.
I AM; SIMPLY I AM.

Master Mural Painter Gleefully Dabbles in Works of Art." In the article, the reporter wrote that Frida told her, with a "twinkle" in her eye, "I didn't study with Diego. I didn't study with anyone. I just started to paint. He does pretty well for a little boy, but it is I who am the big artist."

Friends and acquaintances confirmed in anecdotes and interviews through the years that during her first stint in the United States, the sometimes shy young adult grew into a woman who could verbally spar with the best of them. Being pushed out of the comfort zone of her Mexican hometown to big American cities like San Francisco and New York—where her duty was to wine and dine the "right" circles for the sake of her husband's reputation—gave Frida a kind of slick social smarts. She quickly became known for her ability to command a room; in one infamous story about a dinner in San Francisco early in their marriage, Frida noticed a young woman vying for Diego's attention. Suddenly, she took a big swig of wine and, loudly and boisterously, began to charm the table with jokes and traditional Mexican songs. Soon, everyone's eyes, including the young woman's, were on Frida . . . instead of on her husband.

At times, her confidence led her to push buttons. Another piece of Frida lore involves the time she visited Henry Ford's sister . . . and spent the entire occasion making sarcastic comments about church in front of the devoutly religious woman. And at the motor-company founder's own home, she turned to the auto titan—who was widely known to be anti-Semitic—and asked, "Mr. Ford, are you Jewish?" Luckily for Frida, her husband, Diego, encouraged her mischievousness, later recalling the story and saying, "What a girl!"

Frida wasn't all self-confidence all the time, however. She once wrote, "Of my face, I like the eyebrows and the

OF COURSE, DIEGO DOES PRETTY WELL FOR A LITTLE BOY, BUT IT IS I WHO AM THE BIG ARTIST.

eyes. Aside from that, I like nothing. I have the moustache and in general the face of the opposite sex." She had her own insecurities, and in 1933 she painted a self-portrait titled simply *Very Ugly*, depicting herself using a harsher technique than usual; afterward, she threw the painting in the trash. It was salvaged when her friend Lucienne Bloch discovered the work in the garbage and rescued it.

That reminder of Frida's insecurities illustrates exactly what we can learn from her about self-assurance: confidence is a mindset—and sometimes, you have to fake it 'til you make it. On the inside, Frida was sometimes critical of herself—her features, her inability to produce children, even her work—and as we can tell from her letters and anecdotes from family and friends, she occasionally shared those feelings privately with her inner circle. But outwardly, she was brazen and audacious, never hesitating to brag about her talents as an artist or dress in a way that assured all eyes would be on her in any room.

Frida's fearlessness in the face of her flaws can inspire us to get over our own imposter syndromes; whether we're feeling inadequate in a boardroom or in a relationship, I can imagine that she would tell us—even if we don't quite yet believe it ourselves—to always be our own biggest cheerleaders. We might not be able to control how we feel, but we are in total control of how we project ourselves on the outside. And if we brag about ourselves well enough, we might just start to believe it on the inside, too. Even in her vulnerable moments, Frida was her most authentic self, and she made no apologies about it. In just forty-seven short years of life, she taught us by example to celebrate how bold, brave, and beautiful we are—however we may come.

FRIDA KAHLO, AUTHOR OF HER OWN STORY

According to her birth certificate, Frida Kahlo was born in Coyoacán, Mexico, on July 6, 1907. Later in life, however, she began to assert that she had been born in 1910. And the fib wasn't an attempt to seem younger.

As it turns out, the Mexican Revolution also began in 1910. So when she was older, Frida began to tell people *that* was the year she was born—and that she was the "Daughter of the Revolution." She wanted nothing more than to be associated with not just the fight for freedom but also the beginning of a modern Mexico. And so, as though it were as simple as an edit to her autobiography, she simply changed her own narrative. (It's also worth noting that in the 1930s, she changed the spelling of her name from the German "Frieda" to "Frida," because she did not wish to be associated with Germany during Hitler's rule.)

This wasn't the only white lie told by Frida. The artist often said in interviews and letters that while her mother was of European, Spanish, and indigenous Mexican roots, her father, Guillermo, was of Jewish and Hungarian descent. She'd leave out the fact that he had been born in Germany, yet a biography of Guillermo states that the photographer was descended from a long line of German Lutherans.

In this case, we don't *quite* know whether Frida simply got her information mixed up, or she purposely twisted the truth when it came to her family's identity. (Perhaps she wanted to more closely relate to the struggles of her Jewish comrades?) Whatever the case, we know for sure that our Frida was as creative with her own story as she was with her art.

WHAT THE SOCIAL MEDIA GENERATION CAN LEARN FROM FRIDA

There are Frida Kahlo T-shirts. Frida Kahlo keychains, refrigerator magnets, and, yes, even Barbies. Hop on Pinterest, and you're likely to encounter a Frida Kahlo quote in your first few minutes of clicking around. Every year, somewhere around the world, an exhibition pops up in her honor, whether it's re-creating her home, La Casa Azul, or displaying her work or personal artifacts. Rumors even circulate of cult-like devotional groups who pray to Frida.

Fridamania only deepens with every passing year; posthumously, the artist has transformed from an artist to an icon, someone who is revered not just for being any one thing, but simply for having *existed*.

With the inundation of images of Frida *by* Frida, she has paved the way for a social media generation to love their *own* selves unabashedly. If Frida Kahlo can paint portrait after portrait of herself, why can't *we* take dozens of photos of ourselves to share with the world via social media?

But before there was a little device in billions of people's pockets allowing them to capture their own image at the swipe of a screen, there was Frida, painting in her little bedroom in La Casa Azul. One major difference we should all try to remember? While many of us spend time carefully curating our images to make them perfect, Frida painted every imperfection. Look closely at her self-portraits, and you can see every bit of Frida's infamous unibrow, every hair in the shadow above her lip.

So yes, there is one lesson we can all take from Frida: Love yourself. And never stop taking—and posting!—those selfies. But maybe, just maybe, leave the Facetune and Photoshopping alone. Because no one should love your image, just as it is, more than you do.

What Would Frida Do . . . if She Needed a Dose of Self-Love?

Play up those brows. Frida's eyebrows are perhaps just as iconic as her painting style, and that's no accident. The artist was known for taking particular care of her eyebrows—and rather than tweeze them to make them smaller, as was customary for women at the time, she actually used a Revlon brow pencil to fill them *in*. That's right: a drugstore brand. As seen in some of her belongings featured at the V&A Museum in London in 2018 and the Brooklyn Museum in 2019, Frida was also a fan of other Revlon products, including a cream blush and Everything's Rosy lipstick.

Capture yourself. Frida was around way before the iPhone, of course, so if painting's not your thing, a selfie always works. And don't be afraid to keep trying until you find *just* the right angle; of Frida's 143 paintings, 55 were self-portraits—and those are just the ones we know about. So don't apologize if you've got a camera roll full of you, because, hey: you are the subject you know best.

Make a spectacle. Frida Kahlo loved to make a statement. Beyond her painted art, she was a master in the art of theatrics. At her first and last solo exhibition in Mexico, she didn't let the fact that she was bedridden and deathly ill stop her from attending her own party. Instead of staying home, she simply took her sickbed *with* her. After being carried into the exhibition on a stretcher, she was positioned on her decorated four-poster bed, which had been delivered earlier that day. So if you're feeling a little down, celebrate yourself—in a big way. You've only got one life, after all.

TEQUI

2

PAIN

History is full of stories both well-known and untold that prove the unmatched strength of women. There are the familiar names—the Joan of Arcs and Rosa Parks and Michelle Obamas and Hillary Clintons of the world. And then there are those who are lesser known: the hidden figures who changed culture and history whose names we may never be aware of.

If things had gone differently in Frida's life, she could very well have ended up in the latter category. But her art—and the many letters and journals she left behind chronicling her life—ensured that Frida was a singular name that would be known for centuries. Along with her confidence, there's another reason many have revered Frida so passionately: her strength. Because even the briefest summary of

Frida's life illuminates the kind of unbreakable spirit only present in history's most courageous heroines.

Frida Kahlo was known for her joy of life, or *alegría* in Spanish, and also for her mischievousness; she was a grown-up prone to childlike jokes and pranks. But she was also a woman who overcame polio as a child, survived a bus crash, endured countless surgeries, pulled herself out of bed after multiple miscarriages, and repeatedly put her own heart back together after it was broken by the love of her life. She is also the woman who, as she was approaching death, managed to make a public appearance at her solo exhibition in Mexico. To call Frida Kahlo "strong" would be a gross understatement; she might have lived only forty-seven years, but she survived more in one lifetime than most people experience in several. Still, one of her signature personality traits was that she would never let her pain—either mental or physical—define her.

She experienced, of course, heartbreak from her marriage to Diego Rivera, an almost self-inflicted pain that came from running straight into the arms of an unfaithful man, knowing full well that every sign told her to run the other way. But the story of Diego and Frida is a chapter or two in itself. (Chapters 5 and 6 of this book, in fact.) To know how Frida found the strength to love and lose, it's important to first understand that enduring pain was essentially a normal part of her life—a state that followed her constantly, from an early age.

After the physical pain that resulted from her bout with polio, and the nine months she spent bedridden during which her father administered physical therapy, Frida was soon inflicted with the cruelty of others, particularly her classmates, who nicknamed her "Peg Leg." But even as a

**TO WALLOW IN
YOUR SUFFERING IS
TO LET IT DEVOUR YOU
FROM THE INSIDE.**

young child, Frida didn't let the name-calling affect her. To hide her deformed leg, she began to wear pants and long skirts, wardrobe staples that would eventually become part of her essential look. By the time she was a teenager, she had built a thick skin that could withstand the worst kind of mental and physical agony—which was soon to come her way.

Frida Kahlo was eighteen years old when her life changed forever. She was riding the bus home from school in Coyoacán, Mexico City, with her boyfriend, Alejandro Gómez Arias, a classmate from the National Prep School, when their bus was hit by an oncoming trolley. In the crash, Kahlo's abdomen was impaled by a pole, causing a nearly fatal injury that left her incapable of bearing children and doomed her to a lifetime of operations. Over the course of her life, the complications that stemmed from her injuries led to decades of spinal surgeries, an episode of gangrene, a leg amputation, and a weakness to illnesses like pneumonia, which eventually brought on the pulmonary embolism that took Frida's life.

Alejandro would later recall in an interview that on the bus that day, just before the accident, he noticed an artisan standing near Frida carrying a packet of powdered gold. Moments after the crash, Frida was found lying on the ground, completely nude. Somehow, her clothing had become unfastened due to the impact of the accident, and there was her naked body, covered in red blood—and sparkling gold. It's a memorable scene in Julie Taymor's biopic, *Frida*, starring Salma Hayek, a moment in the film so ethereal one would think it was fabricated for the big screen—but Alejandro's account verifies that this surreal vision was based in truth.

"When people saw her, they cried, 'La bailarina, la bailarina!'" Alejandro remembered. "With the gold on her red, bloody body, they thought she was a dancer." In some ways, this image almost feels like a symbol for the rest of Frida's life—a beautiful work of art resulting from a horrific tragedy.

The pole that punctured Frida's pelvis also displaced three vertebrae, which meant endless doctor's visits and no chance that she would become a mother (though that didn't stop her from eventually trying). She would be prescribed various devices, like corsets, to keep her spine intact. And then there were the stretches of months when she was required to remain in bed to recover from her many illnesses and surgeries.

To many, her fate might sound like a death sentence—if not literally, then at the very least for her spirit. But it was precisely because of those round-the-clock hours spent in pain and solitude that Frida Kahlo found her voice as an artist. Her creations became the one thing she could hold on to—the escape she needed to blot out the constant pain. Her painting may also have been Frida's way of creating a sense of permanence for herself. During her darkest moments when she wondered if she might make it at all, she put her own image onto canvas, to make her mark and ensure her immortality.

In Hayden Herrera's 1983 biography of Frida—for which the author interviewed various people from Frida's life, including Alejandro—she wrote, "Almost everyone in Mexico who speaks of Frida's accident says that it was fated: she did not die because it was her destiny to survive, to live out a cavalry of pain. Frida herself came to share this feeling that suffering—and death—is inevitable; since we each carry the burden of our fate, we must try to make light of it."

Frida's pain ignited in her a dark humor, giving life to the kind of woman who could laugh through private agony,

I TRIED TO DROWN
MY SORROWS, BUT THE
BASTARDS LEARNED
HOW TO SWIM,
AND NOW I AM
OVERWHELMED BY THIS
DECENT AND GOOD FEELING.

who had a penchant for dressing cardboard skeletons in her own clothes, who made death a theme in many of her paintings, and who liked to say, "I tease and laugh at death, so that it won't get the better of me."

Of all the pain that Frida would depict in her paintings throughout her life, her accident never made it onto canvas. From the loss of unborn children to her husband's infidelities, many of Frida's darkest, most personal moments are captured in her paintings forever—but never that moment on the bus. The only depiction she ever created of the incident, that we know of, was a drawing found among the belongings of Diego Rivera's son-in-law, an unfinished sketch showing two vehicles colliding, and two Fridas—one on a stretcher, and a second who appears as a large, doll-like head watching the scene from above.

In the previous chapter, I pointed out as a statement of self-love what is perhaps Frida Kahlo's most well-known quote: "I paint myself because I am so often alone, because I am the person I know best." But the quote also reveals the deep loneliness that Frida's pain brought her, the fact that an accident in one split second determined that she would spend the majority of her hours alone. She even felt isolated from the comfort of family; Frida commented in letters to Alejandro that the Kahlos were less than sympathetic during her recovery: "No one in my house believes that I am really sick."

Frida's letters detail the anguish she dealt with; her letters to Alejandro immediately after the accident show us a young, bored, and heartsick patient, one who desperately wanted her boyfriend to know "minute by minute" exactly what she was enduring. In one letter, she—almost poetically—paints a picture of how her life changed in an instant:

> *A little while ago, not much more than a few days ago, I was a child who went about in a world of colors, of hard and tangible forms. . . . If you knew how terrible it is to know suddenly, as if a bolt of lightning elucidated the earth. Now I live in a painful planet, transparent as ice; but it is as if I had learned everything at once in seconds.*

During this period, Frida vacillated between self-pity (which, like her insecurities, was something she kept largely hidden; the world only saw this side of her once her diaries and letters became public after her death) and an appreciation for life. After her accident, Frida, knowing that her time might be limited, lived theatrically. The world was her stage, and she was the star in a play that she rewrote and perfected during long bouts of time spent stuck in bed with nothing to do but think. Sometimes she'd paint the darkness, and other times she'd open her eyes wide to what the world had to offer—portraying everything from blossoming flowers and juicy, ripe fruit to adorably quirky animals, all in rich, vibrant colors.

It's much easier said than done to make the decision to push through pain, particularly when it's physical. But Frida's tenacity is proof that how we handle it is a choice. Throughout her life, Frida balanced between two approaches to pain: embracing it or ignoring it. Although she might sometimes give in to days or weeks of self-pity and recovery, she'd more often refuse to let her weaknesses stop her from painting, attending events in her honor, or even protesting. Her life shows us that there's nothing wrong with occasionally indulging in pain, or even opening our arms to it. But she also demonstrates that sooner or later, we must find the

FEET, WHAT DO I NEED YOU FOR WHEN I HAVE WINGS TO FLY?

strength to grit our teeth and bear it—and make the decision to not let our pain define us.

In the hours Frida spent alone after her accident, she came to realize her vision for her art: "From that time my obsession was to begin again, painting things just as I saw them with my own eyes and nothing more . . . thus, as the accident changed my path, many things prevented me from fulfilling the desires which everyone considers normal, and to me nothing seemed more normal than to paint what had not been fulfilled."

The day that left Frida covered in gold was far from magical—but it's hard not to wonder whether something almost cosmic happened at the scene of the accident, for in that moment, an icon was born, one who would be hardened and shaped by pain. And now, nearly a century later, millions of people are equal parts haunted by Frida's story and allured by the sparkle of it. And I think that's exactly how she would have wanted it.

A TIMELINE OF FRIDA KAHLO'S ILLNESS

After the trolley accident that changed her life, Frida eventually underwent more than thirty operations. Here, a look at the pain Frida endured during her forty-seven years.

1913

Frida comes down with polio, which affects the growth of her right leg. Doctors have since reflected that it's possible Frida didn't actually have polio, but a similar illness known at the time as "white tumor." Others suggest she may have suffered from spina bifida, a congenital disease.

1925

Frida and her boyfriend, Alejandro, are riding a bus home from school when the vehicle gets hit by an oncoming trolley. The crash results in several severe injuries for Frida, including a broken spine, three broken vertebrae, and a broken pelvic bone, which is shattered by a pole that impales her vagina.

1926

Still recuperating, Frida paints a portrait of herself and sends it to Alejandro. *Self-Portrait in a Velvet Dress* is her first known self-portrait, featuring a sultry Frida in a merlot-red frock. She wrote to Alejandro, "I implore you to put it in a low place where you can see it as if you were looking at me."

1929

Frida marries Diego Rivera. While Frida's mother was never a fan of Diego, her father was for the marriage, knowing Diego could financially support his daughter's medical costs. That year, Frida becomes pregnant—but is forced to terminate the pregnancy because of her "malformed pelvis."

1930

Frida gets pregnant again, but reportedly has to undergo the first of several medically necessary abortions due to health problems that would make it impossible for her to carry a baby to term.

1931

While the Riveras are living in San Francisco, Frida's issues with her right leg land her in the hospital. There, she meets Dr. Leo Eloesser, who becomes her lifelong medical advisor and close confidant; after her death, historians gained insight into her medical history thanks to the letters the two exchanged.

1932

Frida becomes pregnant again and, after a few weeks, grows hopeful that she can carry a baby to term. Instead, she experiences a miscarriage, a tragedy famously depicted in her painting *Henry Ford Hospital.*

1939

Frida contracts several infections during this year; to cope, she begins drinking more heavily.

1943

Frida's career as an artist begins to rise, but her bad health prevents her from traveling. She starts teaching art classes at home to a group of aspiring painters she calls "Los Fridos."

1946

While in New York, Frida receives a bone-graft operation. She is prescribed morphine and has to wear a metal corset for the next year.

1950

Frida spends the majority of the year in the hospital, undergoing seven operations for spinal issues as well as treatment for a severe infection that resulted from the bone grafts.

1953

To deal with an increasingly serious case of gangrene, surgeons amputate Frida's leg below the knee.

1954

In June, Frida comes down with an acute case of bronchial pneumonia, leading to another prescription of bed rest. In July, against doctor's orders, she leaves home to participate in a demonstration against North American intervention in Guatemala. On July 13, still sick with pneumonia, Frida Kahlo passes away in bed at La Casa Azul. Her official cause of death is a pulmonary embolism, though many have speculated she might have committed suicide with a drug overdose. (Her husband, Diego, vehemently denied those claims.)

What Would Frida Do . . . if She Needed to Find Her Inner Strength?

Frida had a clear knowledge and understanding that life had dealt her a dismal deck of cards, and she simply must accept it—so she did. If you're looking to find your own dose of Frida-like strength . . .

Find a creative outlet. Frida's outlet was the canvas, the place where she unleashed her darkest emotions, even the ones she couldn't say out loud. If you're not much of a painter or don't consider yourself creative, you can take another note from Frida's book and write your feelings in letters—or emails, or text messages—to friends or family, or chronicle them in a journal or diary.

Raise a glass. Despite her illnesses, Frida Kahlo loved partying, dancing, mariachi, and tequila. The latter helped to keep her strong during her lowest moments. She loved the liquor of her native country and was known to out-drink men twice her size. Of course, many would have called Frida an alcoholic—and she even called herself one. So although excessive imbibing is never the answer, sometimes if you're looking for a boost, a shot of tequila just might do the trick. But of course, do so safely and responsibly.

Be vulnerable. Take one look at Frida's artwork and the honesty with which she painted, and you will see that she never shied away from being vulnerable. That is also clear from her many personal letters and diaries, particularly the ones she kept during the last three years of her life, which documented the pain she endured almost every hour of the day. In fact, perhaps that was exactly what helped her to stay strong, as though by admitting her vulnerabilities—whether on canvas or to those she loved—she could afterward gather herself up to stand up tall.

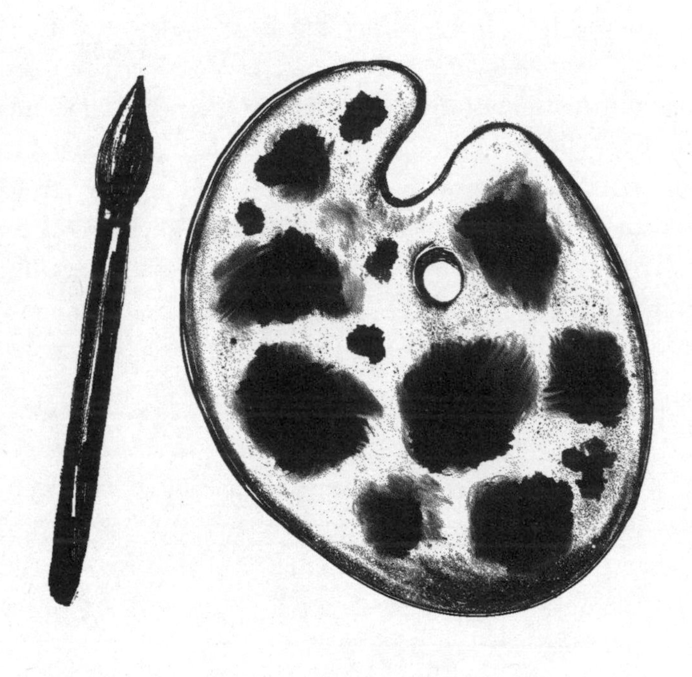

3

CREATIVITY

Creatives love to joke that our homes are never more organized than when we have a deadline. In the days leading up to writing this chapter, I frantically cleaned my New York City studio apartment, finding constant distractions to avoid writing. Procrastination at its finest. Because in order to *write* about creativity and inspiration, one must be inspired—right?

Through it all, I imagined Frida shaking her head at the silly girl who is forcing creativity upon herself instead of letting it happen naturally. As I've tried to avoid her, she has—quite literally—followed me. During a night I spent out with friends, Frida's face gazed at me knowingly from a mural on a restaurant wall. After the Saturday brunch I attended instead of spending the afternoon writing, a van drove by with a colorful illustration of Frida and Diego on its side. Smack dab in the middle of a couch session spent scrolling through dozens of movies to watch, one of the first options that popped up? Salma Hayek's *Frida*.

"Okay, okay, I get it!" I wanted to yell at her. "But I'm stuck. How can *I* know what inspired you and take some of that energy for myself? How did *you* find the spark inside to create some of the most marvelous and memorable works of art our culture has ever seen?"

I'd love to imagine that Frida's wisdom on channeling creativity would include advising me to take a walk outside to soak in the colors and scents around me—to breathe in the natural beauty of the world and spin all my observations into lyrical gold. But the reality is that her answer probably would have been the complete opposite: it's more likely that Frida would have simply suggested that I lock myself in a room with my darkest feelings, fears, and a little tequila . . . and just *do it*.

The key to this artist's creativity is right in front of us, in the story of her life. Frida Kahlo's imagination didn't just descend on her out of nowhere; it was born out of, frankly, boredom, and later, necessity. The lengthy amount of time she spent in bed after the trolley accident is what first inspired Frida to pick up a paintbrush simply to occupy herself. From there, her pain and struggles—both mental and physical—ended up on the canvas throughout her life, a life of expression that meant Frida's deepest feelings were translated via paintbrush onto an easel.

Her husband, Diego, would one day describe her work in an essay this way: "I recommend her to you, not as a husband, but as an enthusiastic admirer of her work, acid and tender, hard as steel and delicate and fine as a butterfly's

**THE ONLY THING
I KNOW IS THAT I PAINT
BECAUSE I NEED TO,
AND I PAINT WHATEVER PASSES
THROUGH MY HEAD WITHOUT
ANY OTHER CONSIDERATION.**

wing, loveable as a beautiful smile, and profound and cruel as the bitterness of life."

Still, the average person has a very different journey from Frida's, and we're living in a time when the number of things that can distract us—group chats and social media and Netflix binge sessions—doesn't leave much room for creativity. So how can any of us channel even just a little bit of Frida's own kind of unmatched genius, whether we're looking to write a book, finish a work project, or simply put together an outfit that breaks the norm?

After Frida's death, several of her works were declared "artistic monuments" by UNESCO. But perhaps the most ironic thing about her legacy is that she didn't intend to be an artist. While Frida was certainly an imaginative child (at six years old, she began talking to her imaginary friend, one she could travel with through a door she drew on her wall), she didn't have aspirations to be an artist until high school. After she learned that her time away from school due to her injuries meant that she could no longer pursue a career as a doctor, Frida turned her ambition toward becoming a medical-textbook illustrator, pairing her natural drawing skills with her passion for medicine.

But the longer Frida spent bedridden, the more creative she got; sometimes she grew so bored she would draw intricate creatures like butterflies on her casts. Soon, her parents set up a special easel so that Frida could paint while lying down. Thanks to that easel and her nearby mirror, Frida's infamous self-portraits were born, each one more whimsical than the last.

From art historians to superfans (hey there, Friduchas!), many have debated how, exactly, to describe Frida's painting style. Both during her lifetime and after, most art critics have called her work, particularly from the late 1930s on, surrealist. But during her life, Frida rejected the label, despite the encouragement of her friend André Breton, a leader of surrealism and one of her early exhibition curators. He was eager to include her in the movement, calling her work "a ribbon around a bomb."

Her first foray into surrealist-style painting began when she and Diego lived in California while Diego worked on several jobs in San Francisco. The couple took a vacation in Atherton, staying at the home of Sigmund Stern. It's believed that is where she painted the portrait of Luther Burbank, a horticulturist who specialized in hybrid plants, portraying him fantastically as half man, half tree, clearly pulling inspiration from the works of her husband. (Diego had once painted the couple's friend Tina Modotti as half woman, half tree trunk.) But in Frida's portrait of Luther, the style is all her own, offering a preview of what some of her future imaginative creations would become.

Of course, the label-averse Frida Kahlo would later say, "I never knew I was a surrealist until André Breton came to Mexico and told me that I was. The only thing I know is that I paint because I need to, and I paint always whatever passes through my head, without any other consideration." Later, when reflecting back on her work, she would offer up the line that has become one of her best-known quotes: "They thought I was a Surrealist, but I wasn't. I never painted dreams or nightmares. I painted my own reality."

Unlike the European surrealist artists such as Salvador Dali, who used their imaginations to create worlds far different from their own, Frida used hers to colorfully illustrate her actual life. For other artists, surrealism was an escape, but for Frida, her painting was simply a form of storytelling.

She once wrote in a letter of her disdain for the "coocoo lunatic sons of bitches of the Surrealists," and in 1952 she wrote to her friend Antonio Rodriguez: "I detest Surrealism. To me it seems to be a decadent manifestation of bourgeois art. A deviation from the true art that the people hope for from the artist." Far from wishing to emulate surrealism, she wrote, "I wish to be worthy, with my painting, of the people to whom I belong and to the ideas that strengthen me. . . . I want my work to be a contribution to the struggle of the people for peace and liberty."

The artist is celebrated to this day for the way she managed to paint for the people. Her use of vibrant primary colors—common in Mexican art and culture, thanks to the ancient Mayans, who produced dyes in shades like indigo, red, and yellow out of natural plants and minerals—and her habit of incorporating indigenous culture propelled her to become a hero for her countrymen and -women. And her realistic, unedited portrayal of the female experience and form sent the message that women, too, have a right to express their pain—a message that would eventually lead to her becoming a feminist icon. So the bottom line is that there really is no single label we can apply to how Frida channeled her creativity onto canvas. She was clearly influenced by elements of surrealism, realism, symbolism, Mexican votive art, folklore, and even religion—but the end result was, purely, Fridaism.

Frida never painted with a public in mind. Unlike the work of her husband, Diego, who was frequently commissioned for specific projects, Frida's paintings in the beginning were a form of self-reflection and release. When Julien Levy asked to feature twenty of her works at an exhibition in New York in 1938—her first and only solo show outside

I NEVER PAINTED
DREAMS OR NIGHTMARES.
I PAINTED MY OWN
REALITY.

Mexico—Frida wrote to her friend Lucienne Bloch, "I don't know what they see in my work. Why do they want me to have a show?"

Similarly, when actor Edward G. Robinson purchased several of her pieces, Frida was surprised—but also suddenly aware of her own career potential: "I kept about 28 paintings hidden. While I was on the roof of the terrace with Mrs. Robinson, Diego showed him my paintings and Robinson bought four of them from me at two hundred dollars each." This was an unexpected delight. "For me it was such a surprise that I marveled and said: 'This way I am going to be able to be free, I'll be able to travel and do what I want without asking Diego for money.'"

We don't need to look any further than Frida's art for inspiration to live a more expressive life. She painted several different types of works throughout her lifetime, but Frida was, of course, most famous for her self-portraits. Her very first was *Self-Portrait in a Velvet Dress*, which she painted from bed to send to her boyfriend, Alejandro, to win back his affections. It's clear that in this initial foray into capturing herself, Frida was influenced by the nineteenth-century portraits she must have seen by Mexican painters, many of whom were influenced by the artists of the European Renaissance.

Her self-portraits would ultimately tell the stories of many aspects of her life. First, there was her physical pain—perhaps most famously captured in 1944's *The Broken Column*, painted after yet another spinal surgery. In that piece, Frida wears a corset, her skin covered in pins and nails. An earthquake-like fissure running through the middle of her body reveals a stone column, on the verge of collapse, in place of where her spine should be. Despite all this ruin, Frida looks whimsical—beautiful yet haunting, her breasts on display, hair gently tumbling behind her, a white sheet covering her groin. White tears fall down her face. It's one of many works Frida created that portray aspects of the frustrations of her injuries, but in *The Broken Column* Frida captures a lifetime of healing, surgeries, and pain in one breathtaking work.

Her self-portraits didn't depict just her physical pain, but also her emotional pain, particularly as a woman. Frida's illnesses and health battles meant that she could never be a mother; a malformed pelvis caused her to suffer several miscarriages, each more tragic than the previous. The loss of her unborn children is told on canvas, as in 1932's *Henry Ford Hospital,* in which she depicts herself bleeding on a bed, surrounded by symbols like a fetus and uterus, all connected to her via ribbonlike umbilical cords.

And, famously, there is the painting she created that same year titled *My Birth.* In it, a woman whose face cannot be seen gives birth to a lifeless baby. Above the scene hangs a portrait of the Virgin of Sorrows, weeping. Frida painted the work shortly following her mother's death and only months after she had lost a baby of her own. *My Birth,* it seems, was a way for Frida to mourn not just one but two losses, while also reflecting on the maternal pain only women can truly know. As a woman today looking back at her 1930s paintings like *Henry Ford* and *My Birth,* I'm astonished by how strong Frida was and also how brave. This was a time when most women struggled to speak up for themselves even in their own households, and here Frida was, openly displaying her pain—and theirs.

Nor did Frida shy away from finding creative ways to incorporate religious symbolism into her work. One storied painting was 1940's *The Wounded Table,* a take on *The Last*

Supper that featured Frida front and center. It was meant to capture her despair after her divorce from Diego. The table itself, which appears to be bleeding, features human legs. On one side are her niece and nephew; on another is a headless, Judas-like figure with a body that looks a lot like Diego's—in other words, a nod to his betrayal. The piece appeared at the International Exhibition of Surrealism, alongside paintings by Dalí and other surrealists.

But Frida's work wasn't all doom and gloom, and not all of Frida's creativity stemmed from pain alone. Although she was unable to bear children, she welcomed many animals into her life, several of whom end up as delightful supporting characters in her self-portraits.

There were the spider monkeys—her favorites included one named Fulang Chang and another she called Caimito de Guayabal—a deer named Granzino, hairless Aztec *ixquintle* dogs, parrots, macaws, and other birds. In several works, she appears Madonna-like with her animal babies; one of the most famous is 1938's *Self-Portrait with a Monkey*, in which her primate friend looks out at the viewer with wide, adorable eyes, one of his arms placed protectively around her neck. Many viewed her monkeys as surrogates for the children she could not have. In this particular painting, she almost seems to reassure the viewer, showing that she still has the affection and love of her animal children.

Frida was also a fan of capturing the outdoors, often using her vibrant painting style to bring flowers to life. Not only did they become a signature part of her own look (in her adult years, Frida was rarely seen without a string of fresh flowers woven into her braided hair), but they were also an integral part of her art. When she wasn't painting portraits, she was painting still lifes brimming with colorful

MANY LIVES
WOULD NOT BE
ENOUGH TO PAINT
THE WAY I WOULD
WISH AND ALL THAT
I WOULD LIKE.

florals and fruits—and later, the Aztec-style garden she planted at her home, La Casa Azul. Much of her later work is set among ferns, palms, agave, and cactus.

In 1946, Frida told her lover, Joseph Bartoli, that she paints flowers "so they will not die." Her words are not only a poetic and melancholy musing on mortality but also a reminder of the power of art. For us as fans of Frida—a woman who was notably preoccupied with death thanks to surviving many near-death experiences—it feels as though her art is a message from a woman who was aware that she should leave something behind.

When I think about what Frida would tell me as a person searching for creative inspiration, fruit and adorable monkeys aside, most likely she would have directed me to look no further than the cracks of my heart. For Frida, these resided in moments like the loss of her children and her many ups and downs with Diego. But she also had a unique way of capturing one of the most basic of all human feelings: loneliness.

This is perhaps most poignantly depicted in *My Dress Hangs There.* Living in New York—"Gringolandia" to her—while her husband worked on a mural at Rockefeller Center, Frida painted a rare scene in which she was not the focal point. Instead, at the center of the canvas is one of her traditional Mexican dresses, hanging on a clothesline; in the background stand symbols of American capitalism: factories, the Statue of Liberty. But there is also a can full of decaying garbage. One glance at this painting, and Frida's homesickness for Mexico and distaste for America are clear.

After reviewing more than a hundred of her works, I've concluded that beyond self-expression, one thing is clearly the key to this particular artist's creativity: authenticity. No matter what anyone else told her, what labels they tried to put on her, or what boundaries she might have broken with her unfiltered works, as both an artist and a woman, Frida Kahlo never tried to be anyone other than herself.

Though she first met Diego while asking if he believed she could sell her art to support her family, during most of their marriage her artistry wasn't motivated by money—or anything beyond her love of the craft. It was only toward the end of her life that Frida became more serious about selling her work to keep herself afloat after separating from her husband—and to cover years and years of unpaid hospital bills. She once wrote to her friend and medical advisor Dr. Eloesser, "I have painted little, and without the least desire for glory or ambition, but with the conviction that, before anything else, I want to give myself pleasure and then, that I want to be able to earn my living with my craft. . . . Many lives would not be enough to paint the way I would wish and all that I would like."

Yet anyone yearning for a more creatively fulfilling life shouldn't strive to emulate or *be* Frida. While we can look to take inspiration *from* the artist and her life, as Frida shows us, the most impactful art is created when you tell your *own* story. What made Frida's work so groundbreaking—and timeless—was the fact that it was completely hers. There's no denying that Frida drew inspiration from a variety of sources, including her husband's work. Yet every one of her paintings is unlike anything the art world had seen before—or has seen since.

Married to a famous artist, she was frequently referred to as "Diego's wife." But she didn't let that stop her from using her raw talent to tell her own tales of miscarriage, infidelity, feminism, and sexuality. From serious political statements to her unique black humor, Frida left her signature on everything she created, using her canvas to tell her story her way. So whether you're looking to leave your mark with a paintbrush, a typewriter, or simply the ways you give back to the world, do it while being your most authentic self. Just as there was only one Frida Kahlo, there is only one you.

FRIDA AND HER FINANCES

It will come as no surprise to learn that Frida Kahlo was not motivated by money. She was staunchly Marxist and anticapitalistic, a fact that was clear in paintings like 1933's *My Dress Hangs There*, which features symbols of America's industrial system next to piles of steaming garbage (subtle!), and *Marxism Will Give Health to the Sick*, centered on a pair of hands—symbols of the Marxist party—embracing an image of Frida. The work's original title? *Peace on Earth So the Marxist Science May Save the Sick and Those Oppressed by Criminal Yankee Capitalism.*

Yet although Frida had no interest in seeing her own work commercialized, as her career progressed, so did her illnesses, which meant more hospital bills—a financial situation that was complicated by her eventual separation and divorce. She often sent money home to support her mother's medical treatments and her father's struggling photography business.

Still, Frida didn't sell many paintings during her lifetime—and her few commissions didn't always go so well. Clare Boothe Luce, a close friend of the American actress Dorothy Hale, paid Frida to paint a commemorative portrait of Hale after she committed suicide. Instead of delivering a typical, peaceful posthumous portrait, Frida depicted Hale's dead body falling from a tall building—and then crashed onto the ground, bloody. Boothe was reportedly so traumatized that she almost fainted after seeing the *recuerdo*.

Given that Frida had several other disagreements about the creative direction of her commissioned works and only one solo exhibition in her lifetime, it's fair to say she had no idea that one day, her works would sell at auction houses for millions of dollars.

HOW THE HOMES OF FRIDA KAHLO INSPIRED HER WORK

LA CASA AZUL

Frida's creative universe was La Casa Azul, or the Blue House, her family's home, where she was born in 1907 and died in 1954. Located in the middle-class Mexico City neighborhood of Coyoacán, La Casa Azul is named for its cobalt-blue color, selected by Frida and Diego after they moved in as an ode to the colorful shades of indigenous Mexican homes. As Frida put it, it was "the color of electricity, purity, and love." Frida remembered that during the Mexican Revolution, when she was a child, her mother would pass out supplies to the army through the windows of the home. And La Casa Azul was where Frida spent many months bedridden after the bus accident—and therefore, where she first became a painter. No matter where she traveled in the world—and even after moving to several other houses in Mexico City—Frida always wanted to return to that blue house.

After she took over the home from her parents as an adult, Frida filled it with colorful items that were odes to her and Diego's Mexican roots, including a sunshine-yellow pyramid displaying pre-Hispanic objects, an outdoor area made of volcanic stone, and a garden of botanicals. (If you walk through the grounds today, you can see that Frida also embraced the juxtaposition of glass and greenery that is common in many homes in Coyoacán.) Her various pets could be found roaming the property, including her spider monkeys, Fulang Chang and Caimito de Guayabal; her hairless Aztec dog, Mr. Xoloti; her deer, Granzino; a parrot, Botanico; and many other birds, including macaws, parakeets, and an eagle, Gertrudis

Caca Blanca (that's Gertrude White Shit, in case you were wondering).

Frida's family home became a popular meeting place, and it was there that the Russian revolutionary Leon Trotsky and his wife lived after obtaining asylum in Mexico. (And there that he began a brief but passionate affair with Frida.) In 1943, when Frida became an art teacher for La Escuela de Pintura y Escultura de La Esmeralda but was too ill to travel to the school, she instead taught classes at the Blue House to a group of four students she called "Los Fridos." La Casa Azul was turned into El Museo de Frida Kahlo four years after her death, in 1958. Today, visitors can see the home exactly as it was when Frida passed away.

THE SAN ANGEL HOUSE

While Frida is most famously associated with La Casa Azul, during the off-and-on years of her marriage, Frida sometimes lived with Diego in a house in the suburbs of the San Angel district of Mexico City—a functionalist architectural marvel now known as the Diego Rivera and Frida Kahlo Home Studio Museum. Built by Frida and Diego's longtime friend, architect Juan O'Gorman, the house was made up of three main buildings: "Diego's house," with a large working studio, connected by a rooftop bridge to "Frida's house." A small photography studio behind both structures was created for Frida's father, Guillermo, and later used by other artists, including Carlos Chavez.

Hayden Herrera's biography of Frida cites a Mexican newspaper article stating that Diego's "architectural theories are based on the Mormon concept of life, that is to say, the objective and subjective interrelationships that exist between the *casa grande* and the *casa chica*!" In other words: the big house is for the man, and the smaller *casita* is for the, um, mistress.

Whenever they fought during the years that Frida lived there, she'd lock the door at the end of the bridge connecting their two houses so that an exasperated Diego would have to walk back across the bridge, down the steps of *his* house, and then around to the front door of Frida's house—which would be locked, too.

When I visited the San Angel house recently, I noticed that Diego's orange-red home was indeed bigger, and Frida's—painted the same blue as her Casa Azul—was smaller. Though Diego lived at the San Angel house from 1934 until he died in 1957, Frida came and went over the years, due both to the ebbs and flows of their marriage and to her preference for her family home. You can sense the difference even decades later: La Casa Azul still vibrates with the energy of Frida Kahlo, but the San Angel house feels empty, melancholy, and almost sorrowful. It's also easy to see why Frida might have preferred the animated, artsy neighborhood of Coyoacán to the swankier, bourgeois San Angel district.

After Diego's death, the San Angel home was passed down to his daughter and other relatives, who drastically updated the layout of the property. In 1986, it became the Diego Rivera Museum, but in 1997—after a restructuring to return the structure to its original floorplan, as it existed when Frida and Diego lived there—it was reopened, christened with its new name, and designated a national landmark.

LIFE IN COLOR

Aside from the content, one of the many aspects of Frida's work that set it apart from that of her European counterparts was her use of color. Frida took the vivid traditions of Mexican art to the next level, beyond even the works of her husband, Diego, using color as an almost secret language for the viewer to decode.

Luckily for us, at the Museo de Frida in Coyoacán is a canvas Frida created featuring some of her most frequently used paint colors. According to the museum, sometime in the 1940s Frida laid out in her diary the deeper meanings behind the saturated hues:

GREEN Warm and good light.

REDDISH PURPLE Aztec. *Tlapali*. Old blood of prickly pear. The most alive and oldest.

BROWN Color of *mole*, of the leaf that goes. Earth.

YELLOW Madness, sickness, fear. Part of the sun and of joy.

COBALT BLUE Electricity and purity. Love.

BLACK Nothing is black, really *nothing*.

LEAF GREEN Leaves, sadness, science. The whole of Germany is this color.

GREENISH YELLOW More madness and mystery. All the phantoms wear suits of this color . . . or at least underclothes.

DARK GREEN Color of bad news and good business.

NAVY BLUE *Distance*. Also tenderness can be of this blue.

MAGENTA Blood? Well, who knows!

What Would Frida Do . . . if She Needed a Spark of Creativity?

Looking at Frida's work might inspire you to tell your own story. Here are a few lessons on creativity that anyone can take from Frida's life and work:

Keep a journal. Much of the Frida Kahlo we know comes from hundreds of diary entries and the many letters she wrote to family and friends. Those written words provide further context for her paintings. She writes in vivid detail of moments like her breakups with Diego, her miscarriages, or even the healing process after her surgeries, many of which later came to life on her canvas.

Build your own creative universe. So much of Frida's work was inspired by the world she created for herself: a brilliantly colorful house that brimmed with animals, plants, flowers, and fruits, all of which make many cameos in her work. Even on the days when she was ill or convalescing from surgery in her bedroom, her works still featured her animals and the many flowers and botanicals that filled her patio and garden.

Be yourself. Of course, Frida had many stylistic inspirations over the years—the influence of the Mexican votive paintings that hung on her walls can be seen in her work, and many of her portraits, particularly her early ones, feel similar to classic nineteenth-century Mexican portraits. But when it came to labeling her work or her style, Frida was never one to embrace labels, nor did she paint with an audience in mind. Instead, she painted from her heart, putting all she had onto each canvas with every brushstroke. She wasn't like any painter, male or female, who came before her, and it's that very authenticity that makes her work uniquely hers.

4

STYLE

It's a uniform recognizable to even the person who is only casually familiar with Frida Kahlo: geometric peasant blouses, long, flowing skirts, chunky, colorful earrings and necklaces, and a braided hairstyle adorned with silky ribbons and fresh flowers.

Today, Frida's style is as well-known as her paintings—perhaps even more so, in some circles. After all, she's had a Barbie modeled after her, and in 2017, she was a Snapchat filter. (Both were controversial: the filter because it noticeably lightened Frida's olive skin; the Barbie because it erased some of Frida's distinctive features, like her unibrow, and because most Frida fans agree that the artist would have disliked being turned into a doll with unrealistic bodily proportions. I'm inclined to agree, though when I study photos of Frida, it's hard not to notice how much she looked like a doll in real life—and there *is* an upside to the notion that little girls can play with a toy that will inspire them to live boldly.)

Frida loved fashion, but she was committed to defining it for herself, often spending hours in front of the mirror and shopping in places as varied as the weekend artisan markets of Mexico and San Francisco's tiny Chinatown shops. In the 1920s, photographer Edward Weston, a friend of Diego, helped the couple get acclimated to San Francisco, where they lived while Diego worked on several commissioned mural projects. Weston wrote that Frida was "a little doll alongside Diego, but a doll in size only, for she is strong and quite beautiful, shows very little of her father's German blood. Dressed in native costume even to *huaraches*, she causes much excitement on the streets of San Francisco. People stop in their tracks to look in wonder."

Some attribute the motivation behind Frida's now iconic look to her wanting to pay tribute to her indigenous Mexican roots. Others believe that her over-the-top outfits were meant to be a distraction from her crippled leg and limp. Still others say that she began to dress like a traditional Mexican wife when she became one. And then there is the idea that perhaps Frida simply saw her body as she did her easels—an opportunity to express herself. Some combination of the above is likely true, because Frida rarely did anything without intention.

It does make sense that the artist's floor-length clothing was chosen to be simply practical, a convenient way to conceal her one major insecurity—the leg that was shortened and crippled from childhood polio, which as a teen she hid with pants and extra socks, offsetting the difference in her height by adding platforms or extra heels to her shoes. Later,

**IN ANOTHER PERIOD
I DRESSED LIKE A BOY
WITH SHAVED HAIR,
PANTS, BOOTS, AND
A LEATHER JACKET.
BUT WHEN I WENT TO
SEE DIEGO, I PUT ON A
TEHUANA COSTUME.**

the leather and steel corsets she often had to wear to deal with the chronic pain that followed her bus accident would be incorporated into her outfits—yet another way of finding a silver lining in her lifelong health problems.

But given that she was a communist who surrounded herself with artists and freethinkers and called herself "the Daughter of the Revolution," I'd like to believe that Frida's style was a feminist ode to her mestiza background and an expression of herself as an artist. Based on one of her quotes, it seems that is indeed true, but there was also a surprising inspiration for this thinking: her husband, Diego. It was Diego and his infatuation with Mexicanism and the colorful dress of women from the isthmus of Tehuana that sparked the idea for what would become Frida's uniform. (One rumor says that Diego had an affair with a beautiful woman from Tehuana who might have piqued his interest in the look, which he then passed on to Frida.)

It's ironic that the style of one of the most influential feminists in history was molded in part by a man. Then again, we're talking about the woman who, at seventeen, defiantly posed for a family portrait while wearing a tweed men's pantsuit, likely much to the dismay of her traditional, religious mother. According to biographer Hayden Herrera, Frida once said, "In another period I dressed like a boy with shaved hair, pants, boots, and a leather jacket. But when I went to see Diego, I put on a Tehuana costume." Clearly, Frida was no stranger to statement dressing.

Still, it was after she began seeing Diego that she underwent a clear shift in aesthetic. In that first Renaissance-style self-portrait she painted and sent to her boyfriend, Alejandro, she appears soft, traditional, and bourgeois; in her second self-portrait, she wears a version of what would become her mestiza-inspired uniform. Her everyday dress would soon mix contemporary Western dresses with Mexican garb, like cotton *huipils* (loose tunics) or Guatemalan coats; modern silver earrings would be paired with indigenous handmade necklaces decorated with stones like onyx and jade. Her hands often glittered with rings, which she loved to collect—and to give away as presents.

The combinations in her attire were nods to her hybrid identity as a proudly Mexican but also contemporary woman. By depicting herself in her self-portraits as strong-willed while wearing the traditionally feminine clothing of her ancestry, she created a character who was both submissive *and* empowered. The kind of woman who would dress to please her husband (even borrowing the clothes of her Indian maid to emulate the "bohemian" mestiza look Diego preferred) but make it her own—to such an extent that its influence has lasted for decades after her death. For years after the event, onlookers recalled the sight of Frida at her husband's side in 1931 for the opening of his exhibition at New York's Museum of Modern Art; while most attendees channeled the utmost glamour in tuxedos, diamonds, and floor-length gowns, little Frida wore her Tehuana-inspired look.

And then there was her ever-present shawl, often worn draped around her shoulders or woven through her braids. But this wasn't just any throw: Frida wore a rebozo, a traditional, long scarf with origins in indigenous cultures. Rebozos were later used during the Mexican Revolution as a symbol of the fight for freedom—and even to help smuggle weapons. Over time, the rebozo became known as a symbol of both freedom and femininity; in fact, thanks to its length (typically about eighty inches long) and durability, in indigenous cultures rebozos are commonly tied tightly around the pelvis during labor pains to offer expectant mothers a bit of relief—and also to cradle newborns. Even in something as simple as an accessory to throw over the shoulders, Frida told a story.

According to Frida's biographer Herrera, the Riveras' neighbor, painter Lucille Blanch, once recalled the careful way Frida curated her looks every day, thinking deeply about which items of clothing to pair and even taking up a needle to add ribbons and embroidery to the hems of her skirts. "Does it work?" Blanch remembers Frida asking for her approval. "Frida had an aesthetic attitude about her dress. She was making a whole picture with colors and shapes."

But what *is* it, exactly, that made Frida Kahlo's style so iconic? Part of the allure is undoubtedly her mystique, a public infatuation that began when she became a permanent fixture at the already famous artist's side. Frida quickly grew more visible, often on Diego's arm adorned in primary colors and her signature skirts and floral hair accessories.

Though she was still a rising star in the art world, she was already becoming an influencer in the fashion realm. In 1933, she wrote to her friend Isabel Campos about her time in New York. "I still run around like crazy and I am getting used to these old clothes. Meanwhile some of the gringa-women are imitating me and trying to dress *a la Mexicana*, but the poor souls only look like cabbages and to tell you the naked truth they look absolutely impossible. That doesn't mean that I look good in them either, but I still get by (don't laugh)."

A few years later, in 1937, Frida famously made an appearance in *Vogue* for a story called "Señoras of Mexico." With an interview by Alice-Leone Moats and photographs by Toni Frissel, the spread features Frida standing next to

SHE CAUSES MUCH EXCITEMENT ON THE STREETS OF SAN FRANCISCO. PEOPLE STOP IN THEIR TRACKS TO LOOK IN WONDER.

an agave plant, dressed in a ruffled peasant top and plaited braids finished with ribbons. Behind her head she holds up a blood-red rebozo, her face pensive, stance defiant. A year later, the Italian designer Elsa Schiaparelli designed the "Madame Rivera" dress, a Tehuana-style dress inspired by Frida's wardrobe. Suddenly, European socialites were wearing the looks of indigenous Mexican women.

Frida enjoyed putting on a show with her choice of apparel. In Herrera's biography, art historian Parker Lesley recalls the evening in 1939 when Frida showed up with her then ex-husband, Diego (the couple divorced, then remarried a year later), for a concert at the Palace of Fine Arts in Mexico City. As Lesley remembers it, "Everyone stared at Frida, who wore her Tehuana dress and all Diego's gold jewelry, and clanked like a knight in armor. She had the Byzantine opulence of the Empress Theodora, a combination of barbarism and elegance. She had two gold incisors and when she was all gussied up she would take off the plain gold caps with rose diamonds in front, so that her smile really sparkled." That's right: long before rappers popularized glittering grills, Frida Kahlo made fashion statements with her teeth.

Just like her quotes and her art, Frida's style is taking on a second life in the new millennium. Over the past decade alone, several exhibitions have popped up around the world featuring Frida's actual clothing, much of which was unearthed when a bathroom at La Casa Azul—locked until after the death of Diego Rivera, at his request—was finally opened. Since then, many of her belongings have traveled to exhibitions from London to New York, though most are kept at Museo Frida Kahlo in Mexico City.

There, fans can view embroidered skirts and dresses, fringed boots, cat-eye sunglasses, and the casts and corsets she was forced to wear for her injuries. Many of those medical devices have been turned into miniature pieces of artwork featuring Frida's tiny hand-painted designs—tigers, monkeys, and the red hammer-and-sickle symbol to represent her communist views. There is even a prosthetic leg that she wore after her own leg was amputated in 1953, but in true Frida fashion, this is not just any prosthesis. At the end is attached a bright-red leather boot with small gold bells, proof that the artist never let her illnesses get in the way of her style.

Walking through one such exhibition in 2019—*Frida Kahlo: Appearances Can Be Deceiving* at the Brooklyn Museum—I was struck with the eerie sense that even though these are pieces of clothing, they're still somehow infused with the essence of . . . Frida. Looking at her worn corsets or the skirts hanging from Frida-sized mannequins and trailing the floor, I feel as though there is something *inside* each of the garments, perhaps the remnants of Frida that still "frame the invisible woman," as Leslie Jamison wrote in the *Paris Review* in 2011.

Her impact on style has remained since that Madame Rivera dress. In 1990, Jean Paul Gaultier was inspired by Frida's corsets when he created Madonna's now-iconic cone bustier for her *Blonde Ambition* tour. Frida's sartorial influence can be seen regularly in the works of designers like Riccardo Tisci and Dolce and Gabbana; for his spring 2018 collection, Rouland Mouret dedicated his collection to Frida, and in the summers of 2018 and 2019, fast-fashion stores featured off-the-shoulder ruffled tops, whimsical skirts, square necklines, indigenous patterns, and statement jewelry that all seemed to be not-so-distant relatives of Frida's attire.

However you feel about her style, one thing is for sure: Frida Kahlo knew how to dress for effect, make a statement,

THE GRINGAS REALLY LIKE ME A LOT AND PAY CLOSE ATTENTION TO ALL THE DRESSES AND REBOZOS THAT I BROUGHT WITH ME, THEIR JAWS DROP AT THE SIGHT OF MY JADE NECKLACES.

and turn the act of plucking clothing out of a closet every morning into an art form. Through the performance art that was her wardrobe, we are taught that grabbing something off a hanger isn't just about putting clothes on your body, but remembering that you, too, are a canvas just waiting to be painted.

Frida's characteristic look wasn't limited to her clothing. Her hair, another of her trademarks, was always carefully braided and pinned into one of a variety of hairdos traditionally worn in various regions of Mexico. Her intricate flower-adorned style is to this day re-created regularly by women who want to add a bit of flair to their looks (or are headed to music festivals).

Every morning, Frida reportedly spent at least an hour carefully brushing, pulling back, then braiding her hair, pinning it into various updos woven with yarns, ribbons, bows, her rebozo scarf, or flowers from her garden like gardenias, dahlias, and bougainvillea. She also went through a particular routine each night, letting her hair down by diligently removing each comb and pin in the *exact* reverse order as it had been applied that morning. When she was too ill or weak to style her own hair, she asked friends or relatives to do it for her.

Julian Levy, her photographer and friend—who had quite the obsession with Frida—captured several striking photographs of the artist in the 1930s: nude, her bare breasts prominent as she took down her hair. He told her biographer Hayden Herrera, "She used to do her hair with things in it. When she unbraided it, she'd put these things in a certain order on her dressing table and then braid them back in. The hair preparation was a fantastic liturgy." This routine inspired him further: "I wrote a poem to her about it, and sent her a Joseph Cornell box. I gave Cornell a lock of Frida's hair, my poem, and a photograph of Frida, and he put together a box with blue glass and mirrors and the presence of Frida."

Frida's love of beauty went beyond her hair and clothing. When her belongings were discovered in 2004, they included lots—and lots—of cosmetics. While visiting La Casa Azul, I was surprised to come across a display featuring the findings of her beauty collection, including still-intact lipsticks and bottles of perfume. The contents reveal a woman who was not just an artist of the canvas or closet, but one who used the transformative powers of makeup to her benefit.

Just as Frida's body was a sort of canvas, so was her face. She was a true artist even in her own aesthetic, and we can bet that everything down to her lipstick shade was carefully curated. (It's no coincidence that La Casa Azul is full of mirrors, including one mounted on the ceiling above her bed, so Frida could see herself as she painted.) The photos and paintings of Frida, an artisan with any brush, make it clear that she took extra care with all her makeup colors, matching powder blushes with lipsticks and nail polishes, favoring shades in the warm red, orange, and pink families—coincidentally (or likely, not so coincidentally) matching her go-to pink rebozo scarf.

Later in her life, Frida made friends with Olga Campos, a psychology student who wrote a study on the artist in which she observed that Frida "possessed—and even radiated—a strange and alluring beauty. . . . She had a special skill for applying make-up. . . . She knew how to transform herself into a sensational beauty, irresistible and unique."

Many of Frida's cosmetics were quite practical; it was a pleasant surprise to see Frida's go-to products on display at the

Brooklyn Museum and discover that much of her cabinet was filled with a brand familiar to anyone who's ever walked into a drugstore: Revlon. Among the remnants of her cosmetic collection were a blush in Clear Red, three nail polishes—Raven Red, Frosted Pink Lightning, and Frosted Snow Pink—and a lipstick in Everything's Rosy. (The shade can be seen on the envelopes of letters Frida sealed with a kiss.)

If you're looking to get a sense of Frida's makeup style, the most dazzling display is in the series of photographs her lover Nickolas Muray captured of her in the 1930s. These full-color portraits reveal a rosy-cheeked Frida adorned with saturated florals, immaculately manicured nails, and bright lips.

But of course, when it comes to her influence on beauty and the lessons we can learn from her, Frida Kahlo made no bigger statement than with her eyebrows. Her husband, Diego, once described his wife's face as bordered by "the wings of a blackbird, their black arches framing two extraordinary brown eyes." Many young women who were born with a visible unibrow would have plucked it into oblivion, but from a young age Frida not only embraced her brows—she enhanced them.

At the exhibition featuring Frida's beauty products, I was surprised to see that, of her many cosmetics, among them was an ebony Revlon eyebrow pencil; also found among her belongings was a Parisian product named Talika that encouraged hair *growth.* So not only did Frida Kahlo have a unibrow and shun the idea of removing it, but she actually brushed it out, filled it in, and encouraged it to grow for the world's viewing pleasure—sending the message that facial hair on a woman can be beautiful, too. Decades later, women now pay to have thick, full brows like Frida's. Yet again, she was a trendsetter ahead of her time.

Frida's style is more than a lesson in embracing what makes you different; she exemplifies turning what sets you apart into your signature. Her eyebrows, mustache, and sharp features were aspects that set her far apart from being considered a "traditional" beauty, but that didn't stop her from celebrating them, both through her use of makeup and in her depictions of herself on canvas. Full eyebrows, a crooked nose, imperfect teeth—it's because of Frida that we can take any features society might deem as "flaws" and instead call attention to them as our most beautiful attributes.

The more I worked on this book and spent hours analyzing photos of Frida, the more I was inspired by the attention to detail she paid when it came to her own image. Her careful head-to-toe curation of her appearance is also a reminder that art and creativity can be expressed in many different ways. Though she was often sickly or bedridden—or just plain heartbroken—Frida spent countless hours considering how she looked on the outside. Even on our worst days, whether we're recovering from a breakup or dealing with health challenges, we can take a note from Frida's book. Every morning, we have the power to choose how we present ourselves—not just to the world, but to ourselves.

Yes, Frida was a trendsetter who used her own body as a canvas to send the message that she was proudly Mexican—and an artist at her core, who simply appreciated beauty. But she also put her best foot forward for *herself*, whether through a swipe of bold red lipstick or a beautifully crafted hairdo. I hope that on your next bad day, you might, like me, be a little bit inspired by the beauty of Frida, and remind yourself that even the clothes you pull off a hanger have the power to tell your story.

THE FRIDA KAHLO HALLOWEEN COSTUME

Every October 31, thousands of Frida Kahlos haunt parties and bars, revelers clad in costumes that are easy to achieve with items found in most women's closets: some combination of a peasant-style blouse with a long skirt, flower-adorned braids, and a penciled-in unibrow. Nearly four million Google results pop up when you search "Frida Kahlo Halloween costumes," and Pinterest abounds with quick-and-easy ideas for how to create your own. Even celebrities from Beyoncé to Danna Paola—who stars in Spain's hit Netflix series *Elite*—have brought the artist back to life on All Hallows' Eve.

There's much debate over whether it's a good idea to dress as Frida Kahlo for Halloween. Some argue that doing so distills the artist and her legacy down to a silly costume—one that ignores the cultural significance of her ancestry and instead serves as a quick-and-dirty way for anyone, even someone who has not a clue about Frida's life or art, to join in on a night of partying. And then there is the issue of *who* can dress as Frida; given that the artist's signature style was so deeply rooted in her indigenous culture, stepping into her dress can easily become culturally appropriative, particularly for people who aren't Latinx or of color. And, of course, a line is always crossed when anyone dares to alter their skin color to match Frida's. (Brown-face is still, believe it or not, an offense that many costume lovers don't understand. If you ever feel you have to dramatically alter your skin or features to match those of another race or ethnicity for a costume, there's one simple rule: don't do it.)

Admittedly, I am guilty of dressing as Frida for Halloween. And when I did, my friends kept staring at me in disbelief; apparently my likeness to the artist was almost too eerie for them to handle during our night out at a bar on the Lower East Side. Would Frida have approved of the idea of thousands of "Fridas" like me skulking through the night every Halloween? With her penchant for dressing up paper skeletons and her love of Día de los Muertos, I'd like to think so. But it's also possible she might balk at the idea of anyone daring to appropriate her culture. Either way, if you choose to do so yourself, make sure to keep the *real* Frida in mind, and treat her legacy—and culture—with respect.

FRIDA'S FAKE *VOGUE* COVER

You've likely seen it on Instagram or Pinterest, or maybe on a postcard in an indie bookshop: Frida Kahlo on the cover of French *Vogue*, wrapped in a black rebozo, her hair woven into a crown with pink flowers, her hands folded beneath a long gold necklace, her gaze clear. The magazine's letterhead rests above her head in a pastel pink, with the date of 1939.

There's only one issue with the oft-shared photo: as with many of Frida's misattributed quotes, this image, too, is false. Though Frida did indeed appear in the "Señoras of Mexico" story in American *Vogue*, she never was in French *Vogue*—and definitely not on its cover. In fact, that photograph was taken by Nickolas Muray, a famous Hungarian photographer—who also happened to be Frida's lover in 1939.

There's no way of knowing where the fake cover originated; it's possible a fan simply mocked it up to celebrate the artist, or perhaps it was created after the 2002 biopic briefly featured a glimpse of Salma Hayek as Frida on the cover of the magazine.

But not to worry: Frida did eventually become a *Vogue* cover girl posthumously. In 2012, Muray's snap of the artist graced *Vogue Mexico* in celebration of a new exhibition in her hometown of Coyoacán, Mexico.

What Would Frida Do . . . if She Needed a Little Style Inspiration?

Frida Kahlo didn't set out to be a style icon; she simply treated her body with as much artistry as she did the canvases she painted on. Here are a few ideas for how you can channel some of her boldness when you get dressed every day:

Celebrate where you come from. The outfit Frida lovers often replicate wasn't created by accident; each element of Frida's look was an homage to her mother's indigenous Mexican roots. Daily, she paired jewelry featuring pre-Columbian stones with Mexican cotton *huipil* tunics, long, embroidered skirts, and a rebozo (a traditional scarf favored by the Aztecs) to show her pride in being Mexican.

Find a uniform. Once you've found a style you love, don't be afraid to lean into it like Frida did with her signature look. Love jeans and a button down? Buy several shirts in a variety of colors and mix up the accessories. Adore a good sheath dress and pump? Why not make that your go-to? A signature look makes getting dressed in the morning much easier—and can actually *increase* creativity by giving you a style to work with that you can shake up however you like.

Go bold or go home. Whether you love the color black or favor vivid hues like Frida did, we can all take a cue from her penchant for going a little over the top to stand out in a crowd. This can mean embracing statement accessories or a bright lipstick—whatever inspires *you.* I believe Frida would think that fashion isn't supposed to be serious, but fun.

5

LOVE

Long before there was Bennifer—or even Elizabeth Taylor and Richard Burton—there was Frida *y* Diego. Friego, if you will. The couple—whose notoriety allowed the two to go by first name only—goes down in history as one of pop culture's most infamous pairings, a tumultuous, art-fueled whirlwind romance that included dozens of affairs, a divorce, and even a *re*marriage.

Based on everything we know about Frida and Diego, there's no denying that their relationship wasn't just rocky, but unhealthy. Many aspects of their pairing are unenviable, and the red flags surrounding Diego should have sent Frida running in the opposite direction from the start. But if we've learned anything about Frida, it's that she didn't do anything small; whether it was her paintings or her outfits, she wasn't one to half-ass any aspect of her life, and that included her love for Diego Rivera.

Diego was born in Guanajuato, Mexico. After spending his youth studying art, he traveled the world to learn the craftmanship behind European frescoes, and when he returned, he became one of the key founders of the Mexican mural movement. By the time he met Frida, he was in his forties and had four children: a son, Diego, with his first wife Angelina Beloff; a daughter, Marika, with his mistress Maria Vorobieff-Stebelska; and daughters Ruth and Guadalupe with his second wife, Guadalupe (a.k.a. Lupe) Marín, to whom Diego was still married when he met Frida.

There are many versions of the story of how Frida and Diego first met, most beginning with a young Frida laying eyes on the six-foot-tall, three-hundred-pound painter while he was working on a mural at Frida's school, the National Preparatory School. Tales abound of a mysterious teenage Frida pranking the already-famous muralist by throwing soap on the stairs that led to his project or peeking in on him while he made love to the various models posing for his works.

But Diego didn't recall meeting Frida until a few years later. He tells his own version of their first encounter in *My Art, My Life*, the autobiography published in 1960 that was based on thousands of pages of notes and anecdotes he gave to journalist Gladys March throughout his lifetime. "I was at work on one of the uppermost frescoes at the Ministry of Education building one day, when I heard a girl shouting up to me, 'Diego, please come down from there! I have something important to discuss with you!'" he recalled.

"I turned my head and looked down from my scaffold. On the ground beneath me stood a girl of about eighteen.

She had a fine nervous body, topped by a delicate face. Her hair was long; dark and thick eyebrows met above her nose." He remembers a young but fierce Frida telling him:

> *I didn't come here for fun. I have to work to earn my livelihood. I have done some paintings which I want you to look over professionally. I want an absolutely straightforward opinion, because I cannot afford to go on just to appease my vanity. I want you to tell me whether you think I can become a good enough artist to make it worth my while to go on. I've brought three of my paintings here. Will you come and look at them?*

Diego was overweight and not traditionally handsome, a fact that would prompt Frida's parents to nickname the couple the "elephant and the dove" and Frida to lovingly call him her "frog." But in addition to his rising fame as a painter, many attributed Diego's success with women to his charm. He was also incredibly confident in his own work, the result of being treated like a prodigy since being caught at age three drawing on the walls. His father, rather than punishing him, placed blackboards on the walls for him to draw on instead. As an adult, he was known for telling over-the-top stories—like the time he claimed to have experimented with a human-flesh diet, wrapping female parts in a corn tortilla, taco style. Diego's circle of friends included notables from Pablo Picasso to Gertrude Stein, and he was also well-known for being casual in his talk of polyamory, often comparing his need to have sex with the urge to . . . urinate.

According to Diego's recollection of Frida's request for a critique of her work, Frida was well aware of his reputation as a womanizer. "The trouble is that some of your good friends have advised me not to put too much stock in what you say," she told him. "They say if it's a girl who asks your opinion and she's not an absolute horror, you are ready to gush all over her."

The muralist says it was then that he recognized the girl—not from Tina Modotti's party, where they had, by all accounts, first *officially* met—but as the young student who used to taunt him as he worked on a mural at the National Preparatory School. "Yes, so what? I was the girl in the auditorium," he remembers his future wife saying, "but that has absolutely nothing to do with now."

Diego also wrote that it was obvious to him that this "girl" was an "authentic artist," so he agreed to visit her home that Sunday to see more of her art. His frequent visits made it clear that her artistic talent wasn't all that he saw in Frida Kahlo. Soon, the forty-one-year-old was spending more and more time at the Kahlo family home with a twenty-year-old Frida, who had recently ended her relationship with her high school beau, Alejandro. Diego, meanwhile, was nearing the end of a tempestuous marriage to Lupe Marín, one that was fraught with physical violence and Diego's infidelities—the last straw being an affair with Tina Modotti.

Diego, smitten with Frida, recalled a walk in her neighborhood when the streetlamps unexpectedly shut off. "On a sudden impulse, I stooped to kiss her. As our lips touched, the light nearest went off and came on again when our lips parted." But a twenty-year age difference and Diego's reputation gave their budding romance the dynamic of a mentor and mentee; while Frida was unbelievably strong and independent in most aspects of her life, she was eager for the affections of both Diego the artist and Diego her lover. She once wrote that Diego told her, "Your will must

CAN ONE INVENT VERBS? I WANT TO TELL YOU ONE: I SKY YOU, SO MY WINGS EXTEND SO LARGE TO LOVE YOU WITHOUT MEASURE.

bring you to your own expression." And so: "I began to paint things that he liked. From that time on he admired me and loved me."

It was Diego whom Frida, newly an adult, looked to for both artistic inspiration and life guidance. It was Diego who suggested that Frida celebrate her indigenous roots by embracing the wardrobe of a more traditional Mexican wife; Diego who would get an already politically minded Frida further involved in the Mexican Communist Party; Diego who would convince Frida that it was okay to marry a man who was vocal about his inability to be loyal.

Still, Diego was, in numerous ways, a positive influence on Frida. She began to incorporate influences from her lover; many point to her 1929 painting *The Bus*—featuring stereotypical Mexican characters seated together in a statement on classism—as her own smaller-scale version of one of Diego's murals. Nor is it any secret that after Diego came into her life, Frida's paintings became more vibrant and saturated with color. In 1950, she would say in an interview, "Diego showed me the revolutionary sense of life and the true sense of color."

Frida and Diego were married on August 21, 1929, in a small ceremony at City Hall. There weren't many guests, since not everyone approved of their union. While some people—including Frida's father, Guillermo—understood the partnership given Diego's rising fame and ability to provide, others were perplexed at the physical differences between this elephant and dove, particularly Frida's mother, Matilde. Frida later told a journalist, "At seventeen, I fell in love with Diego, and my parents did not like this because Diego was a Communist and because they said that he looked like a fat, fat, fat Brueghel."

The physical contrast of a "beauty and the beast" sort is part of the public's fascination with the couple to this day. Even considering her unconventional looks—her monobrow, sharply angled features, and unique way of dressing—Frida was delicate, feminine, and petite. Diego towered over her, and most photos of him show large eyes, wiry, unruly hair, and a large paunch drooping over his belt. Frida was not unaware that her beloved was hardly the movie-star type. For the 1949 catalogue for a fifty-year retrospective of Diego's work at the Palacio de Bellas Artes in Mexico City, Frida wrote an essay she titled, "A Portrait of Diego." In it, she found a rather poetic way to depict her husband's looks, seeing him through what can only be called a lens of love:

> *With his Asiatic head and dark hair, so thin and fine that it seems to float in the air, Diego is an immense, enormous child, with a friendly face and a rather sad gaze. His large protuberant eyes, dark and extremely intelligent, are barely restrained—almost leaping from their orbits—by the swollen, bulging batrachian eyelids, and are set far apart from one another, more so than other eyes. They permit his gaze to embrace a wider visual field, as if they were constructed specially for a painter of spaces and multitudes. Between these eyes, one so far from the other, can be glimpsed the invisibility of Oriental wisdom, but very seldom does there disappear from his full-lipped Buddha-like mouth a tender and ironic smile, the flower of his image.*
>
> *Seeing him nude one thinks immediately of a frog child standing on its hind legs. His skin is greenish-white, like that of an aquatic animal. Only his hands and face are darker, burned by the sun.*

She continues, lyrically transforming what others might consider physical flaws into mythical traits well-suited for a legendary painter. His "narrow, rounded, infantile shoulders" and "marvelous, small, finely-drawn hands" somehow are rendered into tools "sensitive and subtle as antennas that communicate with the entire universe. It is astonishing that those hands have served to paint so much and still work indefatigable." His "belly, enormous, smooth and tender as a sphere, rests on strong legs, as beautiful as columns, that end in large feet," and those feet support a figure whose stance is "splayed outward at an obtuse angle as if to embrace the whole earth and stand upon it without contradiction, like an antediluvian being, from which might emerge, from the waist up, an example of future humanity, two or three thousand years distant from us."

Yup. It takes a woman *in love* to turn a description most would simply label "unattractive" into a work of poetry dripping with so much tender affection that it could bring the reader to tears.

Back in August 1929, Frida was just as enamored, describing her wedding day with the excitement of a young bride—despite the less than perfect circumstances surrounding her nuptials. "I arranged everything in the court of Coyoacán so that we could be married the 21st of August, 1929. I asked the maid for skirts, the blouse and rebozo were also borrowed from the maid. I arranged my foot with the apparatus so that it couldn't be noticed and we got married."

She does mention moments that cast somewhat of a shadow on the proceedings: "No one went to the wedding, only my father, who said to Diego, 'Notice that my daughter is a sick person and all her life she will be sick; she is intelligent, but not pretty. Think it over if you want, and if you wish to get married, I give you my permission.'"

Still, there was a party after the ceremony for friends and relatives at Tina Modotti's home, a scene that is depicted memorably in the film *Frida*. The filmmakers even included the true story of Diego's ex-wife Lupe Marín's appearance and the tantrum she threw; it was Frida herself who had invited her. Bertram Wolfe, a friend of Diego who wrote a biography of the artist, recalled the moment: Lupe "came, pretended to be very gay, then in the midst of the festivities, strode suddenly up to Frida, lifted high the new bride's skirt, and shouted to the assembled company: 'You see these two sticks? These are the legs Diego has now instead of mine!' Then she marched out of the house in triumph."

Frida and Diego's first home was at Reforma 104. Frequent visitors included Diego's fellow muralist and communist David Alfaro Siquieros; his wife, Blanca; and a few other friends. They'd often cozy up in the small home with "a narrow bed, dining room furniture, and a yellow kitchen table" from Frida's mom (who had no choice but to accept the union).

Frida was content, spending her days tending to her "genius" husband, often packing and taking him lunch to eat on the scaffolds while he worked on various projects around Mexico City. Ironically, she learned how to be exactly the kind of wife Diego loved from an important person—his ex-wife, Lupe, who showed Frida her recipes and how to carry his meals to him in a basket, *campesina* style, bedecked in flowers and love notes. "It gave him great pleasure when I arrived with the midday meal in a basket covered with flowers," she'd later tell a friend.

WORDLESS, INFINITE–
YOU. YOU INTENSIFY
EVERYTHING. YOU ARE
FIRE BURNING ALL THAT
IS LEFT OF MY HEART.

The house on Reforma was the first of many places they would live over the years; soon after, Diego was being commissioned for jobs in the United States, and his new bride was right by his side. The newlyweds took on America, beginning their journey to become not just two artists from Mexico—one famous, one aspiring—but a glamorous, world-renowned couple known simply by their first names: Frida and Diego.

In 1930, they headed to San Francisco. In his autobiography, Diego remembered that before departing, Frida painted a portrait for her husband (one that has never been found) featuring herself against a skyline; when the couple landed in San Francisco, he was "almost frightened to realize her imagined city was the very one we were seeing now for the first time." Of course, while Diego basked in the recognition of his work in a new country, Frida was less thrilled with America, writing in a letter to a friend, "I don't particularly like the gringo people . . . they are boring and they all have faces like unbaked rolls (especially the older women)."

In 1931—over a year and a half into their marriage—Frida painted what would become the couple's wedding portrait, one that, even until the end of her life, was a telling depiction of Frida's marriage through her own eyes. For *Frida and Diego Rivera*, Frida wrote a simple inscription: "Here you see us, Me Frieda Kahlo, with my beloved husband Diego Rivera. I painted these portraits in the beautiful city of San Francisco California for our friend Mr. Albert Bender, and it was in the month of April in the year 1931."

In the folk-style portrait of the newlyweds, viewers can find several not-so-hidden messages. First, there is the posture of her gigantic husband, who towers over Frida's diminutive figure. While her stance appears to be all about her husband—docile, feminine, clad in traditional Mexican garb, her stature showing the perfect, doting wife—Diego's body faces away from his significant other. He's clearly distracted and perhaps even uninterested. In his hand is, of course, his other true love: his paintbrushes. Art historians have also pointed out that the outline of the couple seems to follow the shape of the letter *D*, for Diego—another tribute from the wife to her husband.

On the surface, this might appear to be a portrait created by a dedicated wife presenting her genius spouse, but look closer and you'll see a knowing twinkle in Frida's eye. It's as if she's telling the viewer, *He might think he wears the pants in this relationship, but underneath this skirt, it's really me.* Despite their twenty-one-year age difference and Frida's respect for Diego as her art mentor of sorts, in many ways Frida's love for Diego was quite maternal. Yes, she slid easily into the role of submissive Mexican wife, taking her husband basket lunches while he toiled away on various mural projects; but she also cared deeply about his well-being, doing anything to make him happy—even, reportedly, giving him nightly baths with floating toys as though he were a child. She once wrote in her journal, "At every moment he is my child, my child born every moment, diary, from myself."

Her motherly love for her husband is also apparent in a letter she wrote to her friend and doctor, Leo Eloesser, in 1931. Not long after returning to Coyoacán from San Francisco that June, she skimmed over her various health issues to express her concern about Diego:

> *We have arrived safely in this country of enchiladas and fried beans—Diego is already working in the Palace. He has had something the matter with his mouth and what's*

more he is very tired. I would like, if you write to him, that you tell him that it is necessary for his health for him to rest a little, since if he keeps on working like this he is going to die, don't tell him that I told you that he is working so much, but tell him that I told you that it is absolutely necessary for him to rest a little. I would be most grateful to you.

It was a dynamic that would last, even after Frida and Diego got divorced and then back together, and even through Frida's many illnesses, when she was the one who needed to be doted on. In her 1949 painting *The Love Embrace of the Universe, the Earth (Mexico), Diego, Me, and Señor Xolotl*, Frida—herself embraced by the Mexican earth—cradles a naked Diego in her lap, his third eye open and looking straight at the viewer. That same year, in her essay "Portrait of Diego," Frida wrote, "Women—I among them—always would want to hold him in their arms like a new-born baby."

But the love between Diego and Frida was not one-sided; despite his unapologetic philandering, in his own way Diego loved Frida deeply. At La Casa Azul, there's no shortage of letters written from Diego to his "Child of my eyes" and covered in drawings of his lips. And it was Diego who was by Frida's side through her countless illnesses. In a 1932 letter to her mother, Matilde, Frida wrote:

And Diego also, you know, in spite of apparently never caring and just wanting to be painting and painting, loves me a lot and is a very good person. I suppose all men are equally useless when it comes to illnesses, don't you think? But he is magnificent with me. I'm the one who is too demanding sometimes and takes advantage, and I get into frightfully bad moods, but I'll get over that as time goes by.

It was also Diego who was a wreck when his wife had to spend thirteen days in the hospital after the miscarriage of their child. Their friend Lucienne recalled being woken up in the middle of the night to hear Frida's cries of despair as a pale Diego rushed in, disheveled, to ask her to call an ambulance. Later, Lucienne says Diego was "tired all day," commenting that "for women to stand the pain of childbirth, they must be far superior to men." In Frida's infamous painting *Henry Ford Hospital*, which depicted her miscarriage, she prominently featured a lavender orchid given to her by her husband. Frida said, "Diego gave it to me in the hospital. When I painted it, I had the idea of a sexual thing mixed with the sentimental."

In September 1932, Frida traveled back to Mexico after receiving word that her mother was dying, suffering from gallstones and breast cancer. Diego wrote in a letter to his grieving wife:

> *I am very sad here without you, like you I can't even sleep and I hardly take my head away from work. I don't even know what to do without being able to see you, I was sure that I had not loved any woman as I love the chiquita but not until now that she has left me did I know how much I really love her she already knows that she is more than my life, now I know, because really without you this life does not matter to me more than approximately two peanuts at most.*

In his autobiography, *My Art, My Life*, Diego called Frida "the most important fact in my life."

Of course, many people doubt Diego's love for Frida—he was a known womanizer who had numerous extramarital affairs that were quite public, even an affair with his wife's *sister* Cristina. He could be quite cruel and particularly dismissive and inattentive when he was working; many friends reported that in addition to Frida's physical struggles to have a child, Diego purposely made it difficult because he was simply uninterested in having a child with her, given his existing children from previous relationships.

After her husband's months-long relationship with her sister, a brokenhearted Frida still ended up back with him by the end of 1935. For many years, if they weren't exactly a portrait of marital bliss, they led a full life together in the San Angel house, which quickly became a hub for artists and creatives from around the world. But for Frida, the damage from Diego's affair with Cristina had been done, and Diego was clearly incapable of changing; in 1939, the couple filed for divorce. To friends and in interviews, Frida simply said that after she had returned from her first successful art exhibition in New York, the couple began experiencing "difficulties." In his autobiography, Diego would detail why it was his love for his wife that led him to decide a divorce might be in both of their best interests:

> *I never was . . . a faithful husband, even with Frida. As with Angelina and Lupe, I indulged my caprices and had affairs. Now, moved by the extremity of Frida's condition, I began taking stock of myself as a marriage partner. I found very little which could be said in my favor. And yet I knew I could not change. Once, in discovering that I was having an affair with her best friend, Frida left me, only to return with somewhat diminished pride but undiminished love. I loved her too much to want to cause her suffering, and to spare her further torments, I decided to separate from her.*

But even divorce couldn't keep Frida and Diego apart. Although the two remained unmarried for a year, they were never truly distant; they exchanged letters, and Frida continued to handle many of the administrative duties for Diego's work, balancing his checkbooks and minding his paperwork. Reporters recalled seeing Frida accompany Diego, his exwife Lupe, their daughters, and one of his latest lovers to a concert at the Palace of Fine Arts. Quite the entourage. Of course, Frida's attendance with her ex-husband, his other ex-wife, and his new love interest meant that Frida was in full . . . well, Frida mode, flittering about in an outfit so elaborate she turned heads the entire night.

By 1940, Frida again lived in Mexico, her illness growing worse. Diego—working in San Francisco on a commissioned project—became more concerned about his ex-wife, realizing that their time apart was the worst possible thing for her, both mentally and physically. Frida received conflicting diagnoses from her doctors in Mexico, so at the advice of her friend Dr. Eloesser, she flew to San Francisco, where both the doctor and Diego received her.

After more than a month in the hospital—doctor's orders—Frida headed to New York to prepare for an exhibition. There, she wrote a letter to her friend Sigmund Firestone about her worsening medical condition. "I saw Diego, and that helped more than anything else," she wrote. A few sentences later, she casually threw in, "I feel a little better and I am painting a little bit. I will go back to San Francisco and marry Diego again. (He wants me to do so because he says he loves me more than any other girl.) I am very happy . . . we will be together again."

She imposed a few conditions on their remarriage. In his autobiography, Diego recalled that Frida said she would:

I'D LIKE TO PAINT YOU,
BUT THERE ARE NO COLORS,
BECAUSE THERE ARE
SO MANY, IN MY CONFUSION,
THE TANGIBLE FORM OF
MY GREAT LOVE.

> *provide for herself financially from the proceeds of her own work; that I would pay half of our household expenses—nothing more; and that we would have no sexual intercourse. In explaining this last stipulation, she said that, with the images of all my other women flashing through her mind, she couldn't possibly make love with me, for a psychological barrier would spring up as soon as I made advances. I was so happy to have Frida back that I assented to everything.*

The couple remarried on December 8, 1940—Diego's fifty-fourth birthday. Frida would later write to Dr. Eloesser that they had—finally—settled into somewhat of a calm. At least, as calm as things could be in the Rivera household. "The remarriage functions well," she wrote.

> *A small quantity of quarrels—better mutual understanding and on my part, fewer investigations of the tedious kind, with respect to the other women, who frequently occupy a preponderant place in his heart. Thus you can understand that at last—I have learned that life is this way and the rest is painted bread (just an illusion). If I felt better health wise one could say that I am happy.*

Theirs was an untraditional relationship, to say the least. It's likely that the tumultuousness of their love was the very thing that kept bringing Frida back to Diego; their love was as toxic and unstable as it was electric and magnetic. Perhaps the depth of the lows heightened their highs, or perhaps the fires of their conflicts somehow fueled their passionate reconciliations.

Frida's unwavering adoration of her husband endured until her final days. In an interview with Frida's biographer

Hayden Herrera, Mariana Morillo Safa, a friend of the Riveras, remembered that, toward the end of Frida's life, she remained enamored with her "Panzon," often lying still until she heard the front door open. Frida would then whisper, "There's Diego!" Safa added, "Frida treated him like a god . . . he treated her like a sweet thing."

When I try to imagine how Frida would explain what, exactly, she loved so much about the towering, unsightly, controlling man who publicly embarrassed her for years with his extramarital affairs, I can picture her simply shrugging and getting a dreamy look in her eye. If there is one thing we can know for sure, it's that the true love of Frida Kahlo's life wasn't actually art, or even herself, as her many self-portraits would lead us to think. No, her truest love, if we're being honest, was Diego Rivera.

Of course, none of us should aspire to a marriage or relationship as toxic as Frida and Diego's. Theirs was not the stuff of fairy tales—far from it. But if we can glean any lesson from Frida when it comes to *amor*, it's to love fiercely and with abandon. Just as Frida was exactly who she was when it came to her art and her style, she was also unapologetic when it came to whom she chose to love—and how.

Whether it was her mother's opinion then or ours as readers now, no one's view of her husband mattered to Frida more than her own. And in Frida's eyes, the elephant to her dove mattered more than almost anything else in the world. While we might not aspire to land the kind of frog Frida loved, here's hoping we can all experience what it's like to be so passionate about someone—or some *thing*—that it "intensifies everything," no matter what anyone else has to say about it.

THE ELEPHANT AND THE DOVE

As is typical in many Latin cultures, Frida and Diego each had very long names. Diego was born Diego María de la Concepción Juan Nepomuceno Estanislao de la Rivera y Barrientos Acosta y Rodríguez (say that ten times). Frida's was slightly shorter: Magdalena Carmen Frieda Kahlo y Calderón. To the world, however, they were known simply as "Frida" and "Diego." To each other, they had countless pet names. A few:

FRIDA'S NICKNAMES FOR DIEGO:

Frog-toad: A reference to Diego's . . . frog-like looks.

Panzon: An affectionate Spanish word for someone with a "big belly."

Chiquito: The Spanish word for small boy.

Dieguito: The diminutive of Diego's name; she also often referred to her never-born child as the "Dieguito" she always wanted.

DIEGO'S NICKNAMES FOR FRIDA:

Carmen: In their early years in the United States—and during the Nazi era—Diego introduced Frida to his friends as Carmen, preferring not to use her German name. In his broken English, he once introduced her to reporters with: "His name is Carmen."

Chiquitita: Another version of the Spanish word *chiquita*, or small girl.

Niña Chiquita

Fridita

Friducha

FRIDA'S LOVE FOR DIEGO—IN HER OWN WORDS

Many of Frida's diary entries and letters have been immortalized in books and exhibits, with most having a permanent home at the Frida Kahlo Museum in Mexico City. Here is a look at some of her most romantic musings to her dear Dieguito:

"I ask you for violence, in the nonsense, and you, you give me grace, your light and your warmth. . . . I'd like to paint you, but there are no colors, because there are so many, in my confusion, the tangible form of my great love."

"Nothing compares to your hands, nothing like the green-gold of your eyes. My body is filled with you for days and days. you are the mirror of the night. the violent flash of lightning. the dampness of the earth. The hollow of your armpits is my shelter. My fingers touch your blood. All my joy is to feel life spring from your flower-fountain that mine keeps to fill all the paths of my nerves which are yours."

"Although you tell me you see yourself as very ugly, with your short hair when you look in the mirror, I don't believe it, I know how handsome you are anyway and the only thing that I regret is not to be there to kiss you and take care of you and even if I would sometimes bother you with my grumbling. I adore you my Diego. I feel as though I left my child with no one and that you need me. . . . I cannot live without my *chiquito lindo* . . . the house without you is nothing. Everything without you seems horrible to me. I am in love with you more than ever and at each moment more and more. I send you all my love, your *niña chiquitita*."

"Your eyes green swords inside my flesh. waves between our hands. All of you in a space full of sounds–in the shade and in the light. You were called AUXOCHROME the one who captures color. I CHROMOPHORE–the one who gives color. You are all the combinations of numbers. My wish is to understand lines form shades movement. You fulfill and I receive. Your word travels the entirety of space and reaches my cells which are my stars then goes to yours which are my light."

What Would Frida Do . . . if She Was Head over Heels in Love?

Frida Kahlo was not someone who loved lightly. Her marriage to Diego Rivera and her various affairs are as legendary as her penchant for romance. When it comes to matters of the heart, there are a few elements we can try, thanks to Frida's examples:

Dive in headfirst. It's clear from Frida's love letters—and also from the famed stories about the couple—that Frida was not afraid to lose herself in her relationships. She loved, and she loved hard, and for her, the feeling was all-consuming, as important to her life as her craft.

Don't worry about what other people think. Frida's loved ones, including her own mother, were skeptical about her and Diego's relationship. Many noted their differences physically, and outsiders figured it was only a matter of time before Diego's reckless affairs ended their marriage. But through it all—even a divorce and remarriage—Frida never let others' opinions affect her or her relationship.

If you're looking to make a romantic gesture, try a letter. There's no better way to find insight into Frida and Diego's love story than to read Frida's own words, and each of her notes to Diego is pure poetry—romantic musings that would make the most coldhearted person swoon. Even if the 2020s version of a love letter is a text or email, it's impossible not to be inspired to put the emotions of *amor* into words after reading Frida's passionate letters to her "Panzon."

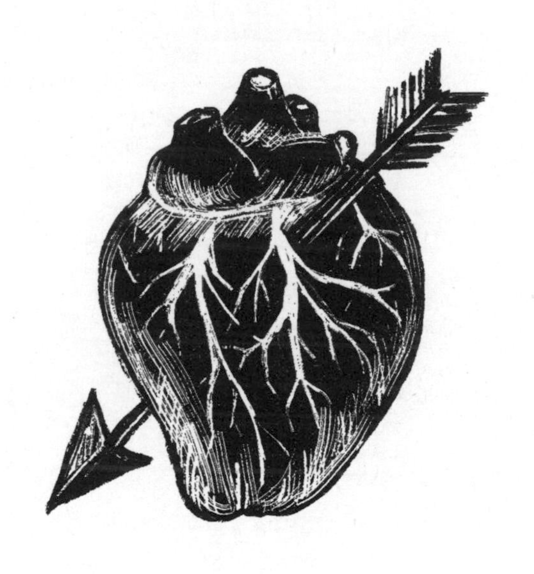

6

HEARTBREAK

In La Casa Azul resides a drawing Frida sketched in 1947 titled *Ruina*. With each jagged pencil stroke, her emotions—anger, sadness, resentment—are clear, and so are the messages. Next to a gravestone covered in the words "Casa Para Aves/Nido Para Amor/Todo Para Nada" ("Birdhouse/Love nest/All for nothing") is a sketch of her husband Diego's face, shattered into multiple parts. Surrounding his head are branches, each labeled with a number from one to twenty, likely the number of extramarital affairs he had during his marriage to Frida (that she knew about, anyway).

The tempest that was the relationship of Frida and Diego is notorious; Diego's carelessness with his affairs, including one with his wife's younger sister, would have been enough to shatter most women. Perhaps Frida's innate strength—a trait she'd built both physically and mentally after years of illnesses and injuries—is what allowed her to keep it together for as long as she did during their marriage. Still, even the strongest of women can reach a breaking point, and that's apparent in *Ruina*: for as deeply and unconditionally as Frida loved her Diego, he left her ruined, over and over.

Their marriage was troubled almost from the very beginning; Frida recalled ending her wedding night in tears. "Diego went on such a terrifying drunk binge with tequila that he took out his pistol, he broke a man's little finger, and broke other things. Then we had a fight, and I left crying and went home." Yet a bad start to their marriage—on their wedding night, at that—couldn't keep Frida from her love for long. "A few days passed and Diego came to fetch me and took me to the house at Reforma 104."

Shortly after the couple wed, they headed south of Mexico City to Cuernavaca for their honeymoon getaway. Frida journaled about many good days the two spent exploring, welcoming guests, and hosting merry dinners overflowing with tequila, but those months were not completely idyllic. Diego couldn't let go of work for long, and soon he was back to painting around the clock, often leaving his beautiful new bride sullen and lonely. Many friends speculated that even during their honeymoon Diego was involved with his assistant, Ione Robinson.

Throughout their years of arguments and Diego's frequent disappearances—he'd often leave at night to give "tours" to visiting Americans, not returning until the morning, smelling of tequila and perfume—Frida's husband was known to try to make up for his wrongdoings by bringing his wife gifts, flowers, or over-the-top love letters. Although on some occasions Frida appeared to be unbothered, on others

I HAVE SUFFERED
TWO GRAVE ACCIDENTS
IN MY LIFE. ONE IN
WHICH A BUS KNOCKED
ME DOWN . . . THE OTHER
ACCIDENT IS DIEGO.

she'd throw tantrums, breaking plates, screaming, and walking around with red-rimmed eyes for days, according to friends and family.

The tension between the two was indeed apparent. Lucienne Bloch, who was Diego's assistant and Frida's good friend, wrote many journal entries about her time living with the Riveras, once chronicling, "Frieda gets so moody and cries so often and needs comfort. Diego is nervous and seems to feel even irritated at Frieda's presence." Frida often confided in her friend about the "hardships of her life with Diego, how irregular and different from what she was used to." But Frida said that if she "held her own," Diego would say "you don't love me."

Diego's worst betrayal occurred in 1934. It was a particularly tense year for the couple, who had just returned from America—or "Gringolandia"—at Frida's insistence; she was tired of the cold weather, the bland food, the constant search for ambition, and the women with faces that looked like "unbaked rolls." A sulking Diego finally agreed, moving the couple into their newly finished San Angel home—two houses, one for each of them, connected by a rooftop walking bridge.

But without the adulation of the Americans and without much work on the horizon in Mexico, Diego quickly grew resentful, sticking around the house less and less, despite Frida's worsening health. In 1934 alone, she had her appendix removed, surgery for the never-ending problems with her foot, and a medically necessary abortion, the result of yet another troublesome pregnancy. Lonely and sickly, Frida spent more time with her sister Cristina—who therefore spent more time with her sister's husband.

After Frida learned about the betrayal by Cristina and Diego, which from Frida's diaries and letters we can deduce occurred in the summer of 1934, she chopped off her hair to hurt the husband who loved her long tresses. The woman so adept at turning her pain into art couldn't even paint. That year, Frida produced not a single painting—but from her diaries and letters, we see firsthand the stages of grief she went through.

On October 18, 1934, Frida wrote to the Riveras' friends Bertram and Ella Wolfe to give them her account of what happened. The letter reveals Frida's utter heartbreak:

> *I have never suffered so much and never believed I could endure such sorrows. You can't imagine the state I'm in and I know it's going to take me years to free myself from this tangle of things I have in my head. . . . In the first place, it's a double sorrow, if I may put it that way. You know better than anyone what Diego means to me in all senses, and then, on the other hand, she was the sister I most loved and that I tried to help as much as I could, so the situation becomes dreadfully complicated and gets worse every day. . . . Before I would spend my days sobbing with grief and rage against myself; now I can't even manage to cry because I understood how stupid and useless it was. I trusted that Diego would change, but I see and know that it's impossible and just stubbornness on my part. . . . He's always telling me lies and he conceals every detail of his life from me as if I were his worst enemy. We're living a life that is false and full of stupidities that I can't bear any longer.*

And yet, she can't help but love him: "I don't have anything because I don't have him. . . . Don't take me for an annoying sentimentalist and an idiot for you both know how I love Diego and what it means to me to lose him."

If you're stricken by this letter, you're not alone. Reading Frida's account of the events between her husband and her sister is both disappointing and a relief. Disappointing in that the image of Frida Kahlo as a model of fortitude is broken. But relief in the relatability of this version of Frida. Instead of seeing a strong, no-nonsense feminist, we are given a look inside the mind of a woman who handles heartbreak with the same confusion and tortured emotions that the rest of us mortals experience. There are no easy answers here, and her feelings are in conflict. The fact that Frida in the end forgave a sister who crossed the line that *no* family member should ever cross, and the fact that amid her heartbreak she was still preoccupied with her love for her husband are both saddening and also understandable. Conflicts like these are messy, and human.

More than a month after penning her letter to the Wolfes, Frida sounds just as grief-stricken in a letter she wrote to her friend Dr. Eloesser:

> *The situation with Diego is worse each day. I know that much of the fault for what has happened has been mine because of not having understood what he wanted from the beginning and because of having opposed something that could no longer be helped. Now, after many months of real torment for me, I forgave my sister and I thought that with this things would change a little, but it was just the opposite. Perhaps for Diego the troublesome situation has improved, but for me it is terrible. It has left me in a state of such unhappiness and discouragement that I do not know what I am going to do. I know that Diego is for the moment more interested in her than me, and I should*

understand that it is not his fault and that I am the one who should compromise if I want him to be happy. But it costs me so much to go through this that you can't have any idea of what I suffer. It is so complicated that I don't know how to explain it to you.

Perhaps the most shocking aspect of Frida's letters from this time is that they offer in-depth insight into a situation that is often depicted as a blip in the timeline of Frida and Diego's marriage. Diego's affair with Cristina was lengthy, and it was also, apparently, fueled by love. It wasn't lust alone that led him to the ultimate betrayal, and even after Frida discovered their secret and eventually forgave her sister, Cristina began working for Diego as an assistant and even posed for him several times.

In 1935, Frida had finally had enough, gathering her belongings and her spider monkey to move out of the San Angel house into a small apartment in the center of Mexico City—a woman with a new haircut and a newly independent life. That year, she drew the sketch for what would become the painting *Self-Portrait with Curly Hair*, one of the artist's most arresting works. In it, Frida depicts herself as we've rarely seen her: with short "poodle" hair, as she called it, her eyes portals into a soul that is clearly wounded, nearly on the brink of tears—but still, somehow, she appears resilient. It's a glimpse at a heartbroken woman attempting to embark on a new life.

Frida wasn't able to stay away from Diego for long; her estranged husband visited her often. Later, desperate for a change of scenery, Frida fled to New York City with two friends, the journalist and art critic Anita Brenner and Mary

Schapiro, sister of the art historian Meyer Schapiro. It was on this trip that Frida decided she could never be rid of her "Panzon."

She wrote in a letter to Diego, "All these letters, liaisons with petticoats, lady teachers of 'English,' gypsy models, assistants with 'good intentions,' 'plenipotentiary emissaries from distant places,' only represent *flirtations*, and that at bottom *you and I* love each other dearly, and thus go through adventures without number, beatings on doors, imprecations, insults, international claims—yet we will always love each other." She attempts to resolve her feelings: "All these things have been repeated throughout the seven years we have lived together, and all the rages I have gone through have served only to make me understand in the end that I love you more than my own skin, and that, though you may not love me in the same way, still you love me somewhat. Isn't that so? I shall always hope that that continues, and with that I am content."

We as Frida fans must come to terms with the fact that the woman was not as strong as we might've thought. She appears here to be in the bargaining stage of grief, mentally trying to balance the knowledge that her husband was a philanderer capable of sleeping with her sister with an awareness that, despite it all, she *still* wanted to be with him, because her love ran that deep. It's a shocking look at exactly how much Frida loved Diego; she was resilient enough, after all, to find her own independence, move to her own apartment, travel with friends, get a new haircut—and yet all she ever really wanted was her man.

Diego later recalled in his autobiography how he came to terms with the fact that it was Frida who truly had his heart, and not her sister Cristina. In 1935, two assassins drove by Diego's studio and shot through the window twice. Diego suspected that the attackers were hired by the German ambassador—who happened to live just a few houses down—after Diego had painted "a highly uncomplimentary painting of Hitler and other Nazi officials." The bullets were aimed in the direction of the woman sitting in the chair where his wife Frida typically sat—except on that day, it was Cristina in the chair, and not Frida.

The assassins narrowly missed. Cristina was several inches shorter than Frida, and the bullets flew right over her head. Diego was struck by the realization that "the would-be assassins had thought that by killing Frida they could hurt me infinitely more than if they struck at me. In this respect, they were absolutely right." Afterward, Cristina—whom Diego wrote in his autobiography was "hot with rage"—grabbed one of his guns and chased after the assassins, shooting one in the leg before police arrived. The men managed to escape prison and fled to Acapulco—where they were soon found hanged. Although Diego maintained he had nothing to do with their deaths, he "was not unhappy others had taken the task upon themselves."

Frida and Diego stayed in touch during their separation. Despite their individual affairs—including Diego's ongoing liaison with Cristina—they'd visit one another or have lunch together, and Frida wrote him frequently from New York. So perhaps it should not be surprising that, following the assassination attempt, Frida returned from New York to reconcile with her husband, forgiving him for his infidelity with her own sister. Soon she had moved back into the San Angel house, where the couple slowly settled into their old routine of living together but separately, as "Frida y Diego." The transition appeared to be full of activity. Their home became a popular social stop for well-knowns ranging from artists and photographers to film starlets (Dolores del Río) and politicians (President of Mexico Lázaro Cárdenas), who dropped by for gossip, laughter, tequila, and a few servings of Frida's cook's *pozole*. For two years during their reconciliation, the Riveras were kept busy hosting anti-Stalinist and Soviet Union exile Leon Trotsky and his wife, Natalia, at the Blue House, where the two sought asylum.

But Diego and Frida's reunion didn't last forever. In 1939, after years of affairs—including a few on Frida's part, though how many of them Diego knew about we can't be sure—and increasing tension, the couple divorced. That October, Frida wrote in a letter to her friend and lover Nickolas Muray:

> *Two weeks ago we began the divorce. I love Diego, you must understand that this* [sic] *troubles will never end in my life, but after the last fight I had with him (by phone) because it is almost a month that I don't see him, I understood that for him it is much better to leave me. He told me the worst things you can imagine and the dirtiest insults I ever expected from him. . . . Now I feel so rotten and lonely that it seems to me that nobody in the world has suffer* [sic] *the way I do, but of course it will be different I hope in a few months.*

But Frida never did truly feel "different." Despite her attempts at independence and the rise of her career as an artist thanks to successful exhibitions of her work in New York and Paris, in both her letters and her paintings over the next year, her pain is apparent, and she was deeply lonely. She wrote to Muray, "I don't want to see anyone that is near

Diego. . . . I don't see anybody. I am almost all day in my house."

Many art historians—and Diego himself—noted that some of Frida's best work happened during their year apart. She produced some of her most famous paintings, including *The Two Fridas.* Like nearly every work she'd created since the trolley accident of her teen years, these paintings showcase Frida's unique way of transforming her pain into art—art that any human who has ever experienced heartbreak, betrayal, loneliness, or all of the above can relate to with a single glimpse.

The separation lasted a year, until Diego—moved by his ex-wife's bad health and the realization that they were better together than apart—asked Frida for her hand in marriage, again . . . several times. She did, of course, eventually give in, and on Diego's fifty-fourth birthday, in 1940, the two remarried under several conditions from Frida, including that they would no longer sleep together. This seemed to be Frida's final stage of grief: acceptance. The Riveras' friend Bertram Wolfe wrote in his biography of Diego, "Despite quarrels, brutality, deeds of spite, even a divorce, in the depths of their beings they continued to give first place to each other. Or rather, to him she came first after his painting and after his dramatizing of his life as a succession of legends, but to her he occupied first place, even before her art." It was clear to Wolfe that Frida loved Diego and had to find a way to continue doing so: "To his great gifts, she held, great indulgence was in order. In any case, she told me once, with rueful laughter, that was how he was, and that was how she loved him. 'I cannot love him for what he is not.'"

Frida opens her essay "A Portrait of Diego" by saying, "I will not speak of Diego as 'my husband,' because that would be ridiculous. Diego has never been, nor will he ever be, anyone's 'husband.'" Later in the piece, she writes:

> *Perhaps you expect to hear laments from me of "how much one suffers" living with a man like Diego. But I don't believe the banks of a river suffer from letting it flow between them, nor that the earth suffers because it rains, nor that the atom suffers from releasing its energy for me, everything has a natural compensation. In my role, difficult and obscure, as ally to an extraordinary being, I enjoy the reward of a spot of green in a mass of red: the reward of equilibrium.*

Poetically at peace, or at least seeming to be, she continues:

> *The sorrows and joys of regular life in this lie-infested society in which I live are not my sorrows and joys. If I have prejudices and am wounded by the actions of others, even those of Diego Rivera, I accept responsibility for my inability to see clearly, and if I don't have them, I have to accept that it is natural for red blood cells to fight against white ones without the slightest prejudice and that this phenomenon only signifies health.*

Frida's heartbreaks weren't caused only by Diego or the other men in her life. One of her biggest sorrows was that she was never able to become a mother. Frida suffered several miscarriages, all the result of her body's inability to bear children due to her various health issues. Some of the miscarriages happened on their own; others were induced by abortions at her doctors' recommendations. Her fractured

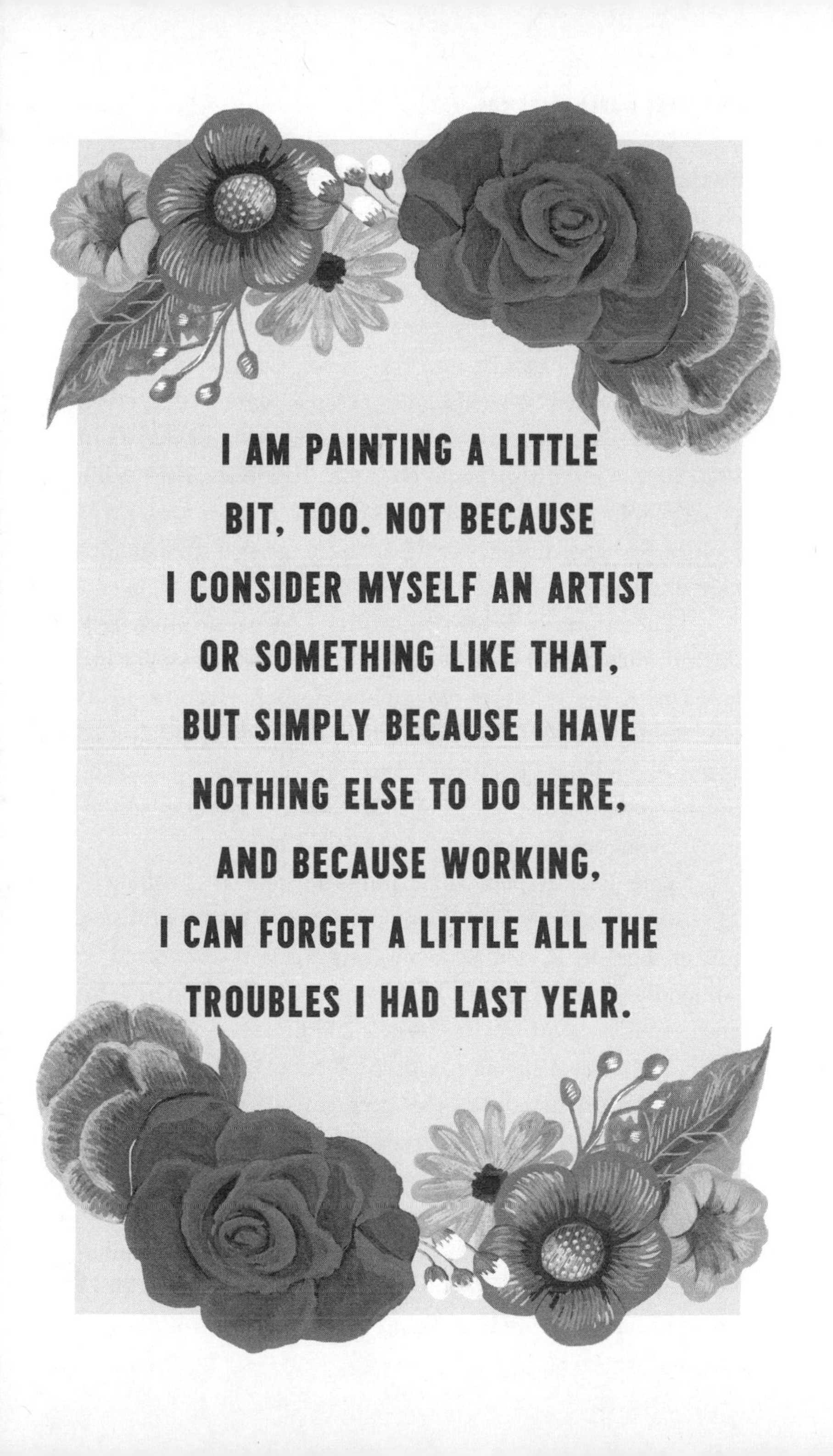
I AM PAINTING A LITTLE
BIT, TOO. NOT BECAUSE
I CONSIDER MYSELF AN ARTIST
OR SOMETHING LIKE THAT,
BUT SIMPLY BECAUSE I HAVE
NOTHING ELSE TO DO HERE,
AND BECAUSE WORKING,
I CAN FORGET A LITTLE ALL THE
TROUBLES I HAD LAST YEAR.

pelvis had never properly healed and reformed, making childbearing impossible.

Soon after the bus accident in 1925, a doctor told her that she had little chance of ever becoming a mother. She created a baptism card for the imaginary son she wished she could have brought into the world. On the note—later found among her journals and personal letters—she wrote, "Leonardo, born in the red cross in the year of our Lord 1925 in the month of September and baptized in the Villa of Coyoacán in the following year. His mother was Frida Kahlo, his godparents were Isabel Campos and Alejandro Gómez Arias."

The effects of Frida's infertility first became apparent during what should have been the honeymoon period for her and Diego. According to biographer Hayden Herrera, Frida later told a friend, "We could not have a child, and I cried inconsolably, but I distracted myself by cooking, dusting the house, sometimes by painting, and every day going to accompany Diego on the scaffold."

One loss in particular, immortalized in the famous 1932 painting *Henry Ford Hospital*, seemed to take the biggest toll on her. In it, a naked, bleeding Frida is connected by ribbonlike umbilical cords to symbols including a male fetus and a snail—meant to symbolize the slowness of her miscarriage, which kept her in the hospital for thirteen days.

Frida predicted that this pregnancy, like her previous ones, would end in a miscarriage, and so to take some control of the situation she tried to abort the baby by ingesting quinine. But when she remained pregnant, she began to hope that she could finally give birth to her own "Dieguito." Still, the stubborn Frida had trouble sticking to her doctor's order of bed rest, often avoiding visiting the doctor because she knew he would tell her—as she put it—"I can't do this, I can't do that, and that's a lot of bunk."

During the pregnancy, Lucienne Bloch, Diego's assistant and Frida's friend, stayed at the couple's home in Detroit to keep Frida company while her husband toiled away on his mural project. On July 4, Lucienne wrote a heartbreaking recollection of the incident in her diary: "Sunday evening, Frida was so blue and menstruating so. She went to bed and the doctor came and told her, as usual, that it was nothing, that she must be quiet. In the night I heard the worst cries of despair." At five in the morning, Diego rushed into Lucienne's room "all disheveled and pale and asked me to call the doctor." She describes Frida "in the agonies of birth," lying in a pool of blood while she awaited the ambulance. "She looked so tiny, twelve years old. Her tresses were wet with tears."

Even in the midst of such pain, while being wheeled into the hospital a delirious Frida took note of the colorful pipes on the hospital ceiling. "Look, Diego! *Que precioso!* How beautiful!"

As we know, Frida's way of coping with tragedy was to put it on canvas. While recovering in the hospital, she became fixated with finding a medical illustration of a male fetus so that she could draw the baby she lost—the one who had "disintegrated in her womb." Diego brought her a medical textbook, and she sketched several pencil drawings of the baby she imagined to be her unborn son; the same drawings would become the basis for the fetus she painted in *Henry Ford Hospital.*

Heartbroken and confused, she wrote to Dr. Eloesser, her friend and medical consultant, "Until now I do not know why I miscarried and for what reason the fetus did not take

IN THE END THERE ARE THOUSANDS OF THINGS THAT ALWAYS REMAIN IN COMPLETE MYSTERY. IN ANY CASE I HAVE A CAT'S LUCK SINCE I DO NOT DIE EASILY, AND THAT'S ALWAYS SOMETHING!

form, so that who knows what the devil is going on inside me, for it is very strange, don't you think? I had such hope to have a little Dieguito who would cry a lot, but now that it has happened there is nothing to do but put up with it." She continues, "In the end there are thousands of things that always remain in complete mystery. In any case I have a cat's luck since I do not die easily, and that's always something!"

Frida was so overtaken by grief that her husband and Lucienne rented a studio nearby so Frida could try her hand at lithography, an art method that uses stone and ink to print images onto paper. Lucienne remembers that her friend threw herself into her work, lashing out at anyone who dared to disturb her: "She would swear each time a fly came settling on her arm." The resulting drawing—which she and Lucienne had to reproduce several times until they got it right—is *Frida and the Abortion*. The lithograph features a statuesque Frida, small tears falling out of her eyes, withstanding the medical process of losing her unborn child, who is symbolized with images of splitting cells and, finally, a fetus. At her side is a painter's palette shaped like a fetus—a message that without being able to give birth or become a mother, Frida felt she had no choice but to paint.

Somehow, with every heartbreak that Frida endured—from the betrayals and infidelities of her husband to the losses of several children—she came out stronger. When you read her letters and diaries, it's clear that Frida was tougher than even *she* might have realized. Several things seem to have helped her cope, some healthier than others. Although a little tequila might not hurt, all accounts indicate that Frida had a bit of a drinking problem, and she even referred to herself as "an alcoholic."

But what really helped her through was her work. As she said in a letter, "I am painting a little bit, too . . . because working, I can forget a little all the troubles I had last year." It's no coincidence that some of Frida's best-known pieces were painted at the height of her pain—while also poignantly depicting that pain. She managed to turn bitter fruit into a kind of artistic brew, so to speak, proof that something beautiful can result from what might seem like even the worst of circumstances.

For Frida, painting about her experiences wasn't just a distraction but a matter of processing; this was long before it was the norm to openly talk about mental health on social media or to go to therapy. As an artist dealing with her feelings on her own, Frida clearly had a great sense of self-awareness, which is evident in works like *Las Dos Fridas*, in which she depicts two versions of herself—one before being heartbroken by Diego and one after.

So, yes, Frida was stronger than she knew, and so are the rest of us. There is a lesson personal to each of us that can be learned from any heartbreak we experience. But it's important that we take the time—like Frida did in letters to friends and family, in her diary, and in her work—to sit back, reflect, and realize those lessons . . . to *see* ourselves through the pain and realize how it shapes us. Thinking about Frida's journey with tragedy raises a question I'll be contemplating long after I finish typing this page: if we were to each paint our own versions of *Las Dos Fridas*—two versions of ourselves, one before heartbreak and one after—what would we look like? I think Frida would want us to take our time answering that question.

PORTRAITS OF A BROKEN HEART

Many of Frida's best-known works offer insight into her roller-coaster marriage. Here are some of her most searing:

A FEW SMALL NIPS, 1935

Frida chronicled the heartbreak of her marriage to Diego in many of her paintings, but one in particular captures the pain inflicted on Frida by her husband. After learning about the affair between Diego and her sister Cristina, Frida didn't paint any works in 1934. And in 1935, she painted only two: *Self-Portrait with Curly Hair* and *A Few Small Nips*. The latter was inspired by an article she read in the paper chronicling the story of a drunk man who stabbed his girlfriend twenty times and defended himself to officials by saying, "I only gave her a few small nips!" In the painting, the murderer, wearing a smug look of satisfaction, looks a lot like Diego Rivera. (Frida later explained: "In Mexico, killing is quite satisfactory and natural.") The woman lies bleeding on a small bed, one arm hanging off the side of the mattress, her blood trickling onto a sickly green floor.

Frida pointed out that the color green was purposeful, symbolizing "insanity, sickness, fear." She also said that she sympathized with the murdered woman, because she, too, had come close to being "murdered by life." The work contains both a haunting eeriness and a black humor; we see the pain of the woman stabbed by her beloved, yet we're also aware that this was, in some twisted way, an act of love. The inscription at the top of the painting, which reads, "Unos cuantos piquetitos!," is carried by two love birds, one white, one black—an acknowledgment from Frida that even in the most painful throes of love, there is still just that: love.

LAS DOS FRIDAS, 1939

Frida painted this piece—perhaps her most recognized work—as her divorce from Diego was being finalized. In it, the "Two Fridas" are seated on a bench. On the right sits a calm Frida wearing her signature Tehuana costume; on the left is a Frida in a Victorian-style dress, its bodice torn to reveal a bare breast and damaged heart. The injured Frida wields a pair of scissors dripping blood onto her lap (near her vagina), and the former Frida holds a childhood portrait of Diego. A vision dreamt up in the throes of despair, Frida's message here is anything but subtle. First, the only person she can rely on through her pain is herself. And second, the Frida before Diego's betrayals was wifely, beloved, and hopeful, naïve enough to believe in their love and the promise of them raising a child together. The new Frida, freshly wounded from the betrayal of her husband, is bereft, bitter—and savage.

SELF-PORTRAIT WITH CROPPED HAIR, 1940

By all accounts, Frida was achingly lonely during the year she was divorced from Diego, and as she did after she discovered his affair with her sister years before, she chopped off her hair in an act of rage and revenge against the husband who reportedly loved her long tresses. This time, instead of merely capturing her new cut, as she had in 1935's *Self-Portrait with Curly Hair*, she depicted the process of cutting off her hair bit by bit—no doubt a metaphor. In the painting, she sits alone in a chair in the middle of a room, surrounded by locks of hair on the floor and wearing an oversized men's suit—likely Diego's. Between her legs she holds a chunk of hair and a pair of scissors. Looking at this work, I'm struck by the feeling that by donning Diego's suit, Frida has stepped into his shoes, and in the process of removing many of the features she most loves about herself—her style, her long hair—she transforms into him, bit by bit.

THE HEARTBREAK OF A MOTHER WHO NEVER WAS

Thanks to Frida's work, we can see how distressing it was for the artist—maternal in nature—to never become a mother herself. Here, a look at how Frida coped by becoming a mother in other ways.

Dolls: Frida was an avid doll collector. At La Casa Azul, a glass armoire across from her daybed displays dolls of various sizes, from babies to tiny figurines, as well as a "puppet theater" that she would often play with when she was sick in bed. Frida was said to keep a "to-do list" for her many dolls, detailing which needed brushing or repair.

Animals: Frida was a mother of sorts to her endless number of pets, all of which famously roamed around La Casa Azul. In her paintings, the affection with which she cared for the creatures—particularly her spider monkeys, Fulang Chang and Caimito de Guayabal—is depicted as protective and parental. She also loved her hairless dog, her deer, and a flock of birds that included a parrot and an eagle. In 1941, when her pet parrot Bonito died, Frida wrote to her friend Emmy Lou Packard, "Imagine, the little parrot 'Bonito' died. I made a little burial for him and everything, and I cried for him a lot since, you remember, he was marvelous."

The children of her loved ones: Frida was a doting stepmother to Diego's children, particularly his daughters, Guadalupe and Ruth, from his former marriage with Lupe Marín. She also was known to spoil her sister Cristina's daughter and son, Isolda and Antonio, treating them with toys, art, music, and dancing lessons. Isolda recalled that she and her brother spent so much time with their Aunt Frida while growing up that she essentially helped raise her: "Always, from the age of four on, I lived with Diego and Frida." Frida was also a devoted godmother to her friend Lucienne's firstborn son, George.

Diego: Frida wrote in her journal, "At every moment [Diego] is my child, my child born every moment, diary, from myself." In the place of having a child of her own, her relationship with her husband was often maternal. She loved to give him baths, she fretted over his meals and diet obsessively, and in her 1949 painting *The Love Embrace of the Universe, the Earth (Mexico), Diego, Me, and Señor Xolotl*, she holds a naked, fully-grown Diego in her lap as though he is an infant.

What Would Frida Do . . . if She Was Heartbroken?

Frida's art, diaries, and letters reveal how she handled the many heartbreaks life threw her way. A few coping mechanisms courtesy of Frida Kahlo:

Feel your pain. Frida's detailed letters show that she was very much in touch with her feelings surrounding the pain of losing both her husband and her unborn children. She wasn't shy about processing her emotions, whether it was by throwing epic fits of rage or crying for seemingly endless days.

Tell your story. The roller-coaster marriage—and divorce, and remarriage—of Frida and Diego is well known and documented because of Frida's art. In paintings like *A Few Small Nips* and several self-portraits, we can see the pain she endured at the hands of her one true love, as well as at the hands of fate, which continuously took away her chances of being a mother. She also opened up candidly in letters to loved ones. Even in the face of shame and betrayal, Frida Kahlo wore her heart on her sleeve.

Try a fresh start—and look. Both may have been acts of retaliation against her philandering husband, but after discovering Diego's betrayals, Frida twice chopped off her hair—once after learning of his affair with her sister Cristina, and again after Frida and Diego's divorce. They were acts of defiance, but they also helped her create a fresh start, offering her a new identity she could take with her when she moved out of the San Angel house and into an apartment of her own. Though Frida ultimately returned to Diego, for a brief respite she experienced what it was like to begin anew—showing that one of the best ways to cope with a broken heart is to build it back up even stronger.

7

SEX

Frida Kahlo was a woman of paradoxes. She had physical features and a wardrobe that were both masculine and feminine. She dreamt up paintings that managed to be both heart wrenching and humorous. And although it seems her heart was reserved for Diego, she also had an insatiable thirst for . . . well, people who were *not* Diego.

You don't need to know much about Frida Kahlo to get a sense of her sexuality—it's everywhere. It's most evident in her eyes in the dozens of photographic portraits captured by her lover Nickolas Muray between 1937 and 1948. In each shot—whether candid or posed—Frida Kahlo, her gaze twinkling and seductive, appears softer and more feminine than she typically depicted herself in her own paintings.

Her work, too, contains no shortage of sexual innuendos. Many of Frida's still lifes feature fruit, sliced open and ripe, juicy and inviting, purposefully shaped to evoke a womb dripping with seeds. Even in her most anguished paintings, a touch of sensuality appears. *Broken Column*, from 1944, depicts a crying Frida with pins and needles covering her skin, a medical corset pushing up the soft curves of her naked breasts—a reminder of the beauty of women even at the height of their pain.

As we know, Frida's life with Diego wasn't all butterflies and lovemaking—in fact, after her husband's many betrayals, one of Frida's requirements for their reconciliation was that they no longer have sex, because it would be too painful for her to do so while imagining his many other liaisons. This did not mean, however, that she herself wasn't having sex. Quite the contrary; after all, this is the woman who gave a group of reporters an interview from her bed . . . while she slowly sucked a long, hard candy. Frida's friend, the math historian Jean van Heijenoort, wrote in his autobiography that the artist told him her motto for life was simple: "Make love, take a bath, make love again."

The photographer Julian Levy became known for a series of stunning black-and-white portraits he captured of a nude Frida taking down her signature hairdo. He described her to biographer Hayden Herrera as a "mythical creature, not of this world—proud and absolutely sure of herself, yet terribly soft and manly as an orchid." He also recalled that she was "very cavalier with her men," playing them against one another when she grew bored.

He tells the story of joining Frida in Pennsylvania to see Edgar Kaufmann Sr., who was interested in being her patron. The visit quickly turned into a competition for

Frida's affections, with both men, as Levy remembers it, taking turns catching the other climbing the stairs in the middle of the night to visit Frida's room. In the end, it was Levy who ended up in Frida's bedroom; the relationship between the two was apparently much more than that of a photographer and his subject.

Frida's love of sex was well-known among friends of hers and Diego's. For Hayden Herrera's biography of Frida, their friend the Swiss artist Lucienne Bloch remembered a game, inspired by the surrealists, that the couple played with their houseguests. One person began by drawing a head at the top of a piece of paper, then folding the page to hide the image from the next player. Each player added a section to the body, folded the paper for the next player, and passed it on. You can probably guess whose drawings were the most . . . creative. Bloch recalled:

> *Frida did all the worst ones. Some of them made me blush, and I do not blush easily. She would show an enormous penis dripping with semen. And we found out later when we unfolded the paper that it was a woman all dressed up with big bosoms, and all that, until it got to the penis. Diego laughed and said, "You know that women are far more pornographic than men."*

During her breaks from Diego and also during her marriage, Frida Kahlo took many lovers. Now, I know I probably shouldn't inject my own opinion here, or encourage tit for tat in a relationship. But after so many years of disrespect from the love of her life, it almost seems fair that Frida got to have her own exploits. Yes, she was sometimes the helpless, lovesick, and weak woman we read about in

MAKE LOVE,

TAKE A BATH,

MAKE LOVE AGAIN.

the previous chapter—the person showing many of the same flaws we've *all* experienced when we're dumbstruck with love. But reading about Frida's sexual trysts is a reminder that, at her core, she was a woman with needs, one who wasn't going to let her husband's actions stop her from finding her own satisfaction—even if it was only physical.

By many accounts, when it came to her affairs, Frida was adept at keeping secrets from her notoriously possessive husband (his jealousy was ironic, given his own extracurricular activities). While Diego was busy working (or "entertaining tourists"), Frida grew skilled at setting up rendezvous. Her missions were easier when the couple resided in the San Angel home, where they lived increasingly independent lives thanks to the separation between the two houses. Frida could lock her door to keep Diego out, or sneak down the back staircase and head to *her* family's home, La Casa Azul, without being noticed by her husband.

The secrecy means that Frida may have participated in plenty of love affairs that we'll never know about. It's mostly from her letters—often poetic and charmingly over the top—that we get a sneak peek inside some of her longest-lasting (and lustiest) affairs. That's also probably the reason why Diego kept many of Frida's belongings locked up in their bathroom until after his death, even when the rest of La Casa Azul was open to the public as a museum. Diego knew his wife and the stories that her letters, diaries, and clothing contained, and as much for his own privacy as for Frida's, there were certain things he wanted kept hidden.

Among the letters that were discovered and made public after 2004 was correspondence between Frida and Isamu Noguchi. In 1935, Noguchi was a rising star in the art world, a sculptor who spent a year in Mexico City on a Guggenheim grant while working on a mural. Herrera quotes the artist, who remembered his time with Frida fondly: "I loved her very much. . . . She was a lovely person, absolutely marvelous person. Since Diego was well-known to be a lady chaser, she cannot be blamed if she saw some men." He goes on, "In those days we all sort of, more or less horsed around, and Diego did and so did Frida. It wasn't quite acceptable to him, however, I used to have assignations with her here and there. One of the places was her sister Cristina's place, the blue house in Coyoacán."

That's right: the year after Frida caught her sister and her husband in an affair, she began to set up trysts of her *own* at the Blue House . . . where her sister lived, and with her sister's help. Isamu recalled that he, Frida, and Cristina went out dancing—a favorite hobby of Frida's, despite her injuries. "That was her passion you know, everything that she couldn't do she loved to do. It made her absolutely furious to be unable to do things."

Frida and Noguchi's fling heated up into a full-on relationship as the couple considered renting an apartment for their passionate meetings. But rumor has it the idea ended almost as quickly as it started after a receipt for some of Frida's new furniture was accidentally delivered to . . . you guessed it: Diego Rivera. As the story goes, the man who'd stepped outside his marriage dozens of times—and publicly, at that—could not accept his wife's infidelity. When Diego saw Noguchi, as Noguchi told Herrera, "He showed me his gun and said: 'Next time I see you, I'm going to shoot you!'"

Little did Diego know that he himself would be the catalyst for Frida's next passionate love affair. By 1938, Diego had declared himself a Trotskyite, supporting Russian revolutionary Leon Trotsky, who had been exiled from the Soviet

THERE WAS ALL
MANNER OF FRUITS
IN THE JUICE OF YOUR LIPS,
THE BLOOD OF THE
POMEGRANATE, THE HORIZON
OF THE *MAMMEE* AND
THE PURIFIED PINEAPPLE.

Union for his anti-Stalinist views. As a fugitive, Trotsky had formed the group Fourth International to push his agenda of worldwide communism, with a particular emphasis on helping the working class overthrow capitalism.

As Diego became more politically aligned with Trotskyism, so did Frida, helping her husband raise money for Spanish militiamen and filling Diego's shoes when he was sick (during that year, Diego was in and out of the hospital for kidney and eye problems). Diego was an active member of the Mexican section of Trotsky's International Communist League and worked with the Mexican president Lázaro Cárdenas to offer asylum to Trotsky and his wife, Natalia.

Diego and his network of fellow communists in Mexico secretly welcomed the Trotskys to La Casa Azul, where they would live for the next two years. Diego had several tweaks made to the home to ensure their safety, including adding iron gates and beams to the windows to obstruct the view from the street. (He also eventually purchased the lot of the house next door to avoid nosiness from the neighbors; the added land gave Frida space for a studio of her own and to expand her garden.)

The Trotskys and the Riveras quickly became a crew of two couples, spending most of their time together behind the walls of La Casa Azul for Leon's safety, or taking the occasional excursion outside town. (Ironically, Frida's sister Cristina was frequently their driver.) But since the Trotskys did not speak Spanish, Frida served as their translator and hostess; she was often at Leon's side as he worked, wrote, or spoke at political events.

You can probably see where this is going. It could have been his intellect, his charisma, or simply his interest in her outspoken opinions that drew Frida to Leon Trotsky—or "El

Viejo," as she called him. Or maybe she thought that no revenge could be more painful to her husband than her having a liaison with his political idol. Whatever the reason, the two quickly found themselves embroiled in a fervent love affair, one made easier by the absence of Diego due to his work, political activities, and illnesses—and by the fact that Leon's wife, Natalia, did not speak English, the common language between Trotsky and Frida.

The illicit couple developed a routine of tucking letters written in English into books they exchanged. They met for rendezvous at Cristina's house on nearby Aguayo Street. (You might notice a theme here of Frida using her sister's home for her trysts. I can't imagine that Cristina would ever have threatened to tell, given her own past with Frida's husband. Quite the complicated web.) The two exchanged a flurry of intense love notes, even when Frida traveled for her work. Trotsky often called Frida his "child," writing in one letter, "Little sweet child of mine: My beautiful baby, I have just received your letter and I have no words but to say I love you. Many kisses my child." And Frida was just as enamored, once writing, "Child of my eyes: Today, even though you don't remember, is your saint's day. 13 November. I am giving you these little things so you see that I know every single day of your life because your life is mine. Your girl, Frida."

Despite the whirlwind, it seems it was Frida who ended the relationship. Trotsky apparently sent her a lengthy letter pleading for her to return to him, but Frida wrote to her friend Ella Wolfe, "I am very tired of the old man." For Frida, the initial attraction was lust, not love, sparked by the revolutionary's mind and status—but not his heart.

Still, a few months after their relationship ended, Frida gifted Leon with a self-portrait, one of the most delicately feminine portraits she ever painted of herself, the image leaping off the page with saturated hues that are a clear ode to Mexican styles rather than European. Her cheeks are flushed pink and her lipstick a vibrant red; she wears her traditional Tehuana-inspired look with delicate, dangling earrings. In her hands, folded elegantly beneath a warm brown rebozo, she carries both a bouquet of flowers and a letter. The letter bears an inscription that reads, "For Leon Trotsky with all love I dedicate this painting on the 7th of November, 1937. Frida Kahlo in San Angel, Mexico."

Two years later—after a rift developed between Diego and Leon (unrelated to his affair with Frida)—the Riveras distanced themselves from both Trotsky and Trotskyism. Not long after, Trotsky was assassinated, stabbed in the head with an ice pick. Despite the fact that they were no longer romantically involved, Frida didn't take the news well; she blamed her husband for bringing Trotsky to Mexico in the first place. Further complicating the matter was the fact that Frida *knew* Trotsky's assassin, Ramón Mercader, whom she'd been introduced to the previous year in Paris, where he was working as an undercover agent for Stalin. Because of her connection to Mercader, Frida was arrested by police and interrogated for two days; eventually she was found innocent of any involvement in her ex-lover's murder.

In 1939, just before her divorce from Diego, Frida became entangled with Ricardo Arias Viñas, a refugee from Spain who was seeking asylum in Mexico City. From what we can gather, it seems their relationship was brief and almost maternal. In this case, Frida was the savior, helping the young Spaniard get settled in Mexico and even asking Henry Ford if he might consider writing a letter of recommendation for Viñas, who had previously worked at Ford Motors.

"With all his experience he could get a job quite easily, but having worked for the Ford Motor Co. such a long time, he would gladly prefer to get a position in your Plant in Mexico City," Frida wrote to Ford on behalf of her lover. "I would appreciate very much all the interest you may give to my petition. Let me thank you in advance for your kindness, hoping that this favor will not cause you any trouble. Please be so kind to give my love to Mrs. Ford and your children, to your parents, and also to all the good friends from Detroit."

We know many details about this period in Frida's life thanks to the letters she wrote to another lover: photographer Nickolas Muray, who had become a star in arts and journalism circles in the 1920s because of his photographic work for magazines like *Harper's Bazaar* and *Vanity Fair*. He was a magnet for both intellectuals and women, including Frida. (He married four times.) The two grew close while she was in New York in 1939—a few months before she and Diego divorced. According to her diaries and letters, of all her lovers besides Diego, Frida came the closest to finding true love with Muray. She wrote to him from Paris after they had spent several months together in New York:

> *Your telegram arrived this morning, and I cried very much—of happiness, and because I miss you with all my heart and my blood. Your letter, my sweet, came yesterday, it is so beautiful, so tender that I have no words to tell you what a joy it gave me. I adore you my love, believe me, like I never loved anyone—only Diego will be in my heart as close as you—always.*

After Nickolas ended their relationship—realizing that he could never *actually* come close to Diego in Frida's heart, and also because he had found another lover—Frida summarized their affair in a letter without sentimentality, as though it were just a fleeting rendezvous:

> *Nick darling, I got my wonderful picture you send* [sic] *to me, I find it even more beautiful than in New York. Diego says that it is as marvelous as a Piero della Francesca. To me is* [sic] *more than that, it is a treasure, and besides, it will always remind me that morning we had breakfast together in the Barbizon Plaza Drug Store, and afterwards we went to your shop to take photos.*

She continues, "You will always be inside the magenta rebozo (on the left side)."

Frida and Nickolas remained close friends, and many of his photos of her would eventually be plastered on T-shirts, coin purses, beach bags, and the like, all over the world. While we can thank Diego Rivera for some of the most impassioned paintings about heartbreak the world has ever seen, we can thank Nickolas Muray for capturing the artist at her realest—raw, joyful, seductive, and, yes, sexy.

Some of Frida's lovers happened to be women. And it's the casual way in which she dabbled in affairs with both men and women—without ever making much of a "thing" about it or putting labels on her preferences—that has led to her becoming somewhat of an icon for the queer community. Today's society is finally moving toward a more fluid, progressive, label-free approach to gender, sexuality, and love—an attitude Frida Kahlo adopted as far back as the 1920s. Looking at the facts, it's clear that Frida was sexually fluid, but she never put any such title on herself; she simply lived,

I DON'T BELONG TO ANY CATEGORY.

taking whichever lovers felt right at the moment, no matter their gender.

In Hayden Herrera's biography of Frida, Lucienne Bloch recalls that, over breakfast one morning, Diego abruptly said to her with a laugh, "You know Frida is homosexual, don't you?" Lucienne remembers Frida and Diego casually chatting about the way Frida flirted with the American artist Georgia O'Keeffe at an art gallery. Diego was understanding of his wife's attraction to her same sex, because "women were more civilized and sensitive than men because men were simpler sexually." As Diego put it, while a man's, um, pleasure zone is . . . well, pretty much exactly where it is, women's pleasure points are "all over the body, and therefore two women together would have a much more extraordinary experience."

Lucienne's account corroborates the common belief that although Diego could be extremely jealous about Frida and other men, for the most part he accepted Frida's affairs with other women—even encouraged them. (We don't know whether that was because he wanted to keep his wife busy while he was otherwise occupied, whether he wanted his wife to be satisfied in ways he could not satisfy her, or whether he simply did not consider women his competition.)

Frida's first same-sex experience occurred when she was thirteen. Her gym teacher, Sara Zenil, had taken an interest in the young student, and soon Frida's mother discovered letters between the two, detailing their sexual relationship. Frida claimed that the encounters were consensual, but Matilde Kahlo quickly pulled her daughter out of that school, which is how Frida ended up enrolled in the National Preparatory School. From then on, she openly experimented with both gender and sexuality, often donning men's suits and caps just as easily as she did flowing skirts and red lipstick.

Frida had dozens of liaisons with women, particularly toward the end of her life; friends speculated that this might partially have been because heterosexual sex grew more difficult due to her worsening health and frailty. But it was also due to pure preference, which Frida had no qualms being honest about; she confessed to her close childhood friend Isabel Campos that she was "attracted to dark nipples but repelled by pink nipples in a woman."

As for the flirtation Frida joked about between her and Georgia O'Keeffe? It turned out to be more than just flirting; we know from Frida's letters that the two were sexually involved. When O'Keeffe landed in the hospital in 1933, Frida wrote the fellow artist quite the poetic letter: "I thought of you a lot and never forget your wonderful hands and the color of your eyes. . . . I like you very much Georgia." In 1995, years after both Frida's and Georgia's deaths, the art dealer Mary-Anne Martin revealed another letter Frida had written to a friend in Detroit in 1933: "O'Keeffe was in the hospital for three months, she went to Bermuda for a rest. She didn't made [*sic*] love to me that time, I think on account of her weakness. Too bad. Well that's all I can tell you until now."

Frida was notorious for initiating relationships with her husband's mistresses—and also the women he was flirting with whom she wanted to disarm. Whether she did it as an act of defiance to show her husband what she was capable of, as a way to prop up her pride by proving that she was the better lover, or simply as a way to exact revenge against her husband's flippant yet hurtful affairs and indiscretions, we'll never know for sure.

One of those women is rumored to have been the photographer Tina Modotti, a close friend of the Riveras who had been previously romantically involved with Diego. A complicating factor is that Tina might have been the one who sparked the relationship between Diego and Frida by introducing them at a party she threw. As she did with several of her husband's lovers—former and current—Frida maintained a close friendship with the photographer. But although a love story between Modotti and Kahlo isn't impossible—and the 2002 film *Frida* depicts Frida seducing Tina—there's little concrete evidence to suggest the pair actually made the transition from friends to lovers.

Another well-known woman Frida was rumored to have been involved with was the starlet Dolores del Río—one of Hollywood's first Latin American film stars, who became a close friend of the Riveras in the 1930s and was known for her relationships with both men and women. In 1939, after her divorce from Diego, Frida gifted del Río with the painting *Two Nudes in a Forest*, which features Frida and a woman who looks a whole lot like . . . well, Dolores del Río.

Frida's most intimate relationship with another woman wouldn't come to light until many years after her death. In 2000, Costa Rican singer Chavela Vargas—who moved to Mexico as a teen in the 1930s and often performed *rancheras* dressed as a man—published her autobiography, in which she opened up about her life as a lesbian and mentions getting to know Frida Kahlo.

After the two first met, Frida wrote to her friend the poet Carlos Pellicer, "Today I met Chavela Vargas. An extraordinary woman, a lesbian, and what's more, I desire her. I do not know if she felt what I did. But I believe she is a woman who is liberal enough that if she asked me, I wouldn't hesitate for a second to undress in front of her. . . . Was she a gift sent to me from heaven?" Vargas also recalled that Frida once told her, "I live only for you and Diego."

Frida had several other close female friends who were rumored to be her lovers, though little evidence exists to confirm the affairs beyond speculation. These include Teresa Proenza, secretary to President Lázaro Cárdenas, and French painter Jacqueline Lamba, who was married to André Breton, a writer, founder of surrealism, and friend of the Riveras. Some of her other rumored partners were also well-known, including actress Paulette Goddard and film star María Félix. Both, it should be noted, were mistresses of Frida's husband, Diego.

Murmurings have also long endured about a brief encounter between Frida and the American-born French entertainer and civil rights activist Josephine Baker, who was also reportedly bisexual—a story that's briefly but imaginatively depicted in the biopic *Frida*. But by all accounts, aside from a 1952 photo that depicts them together, a love affair between the two women seems to be just a rumor (though a juicy one, indeed).

I share the details of Frida's romances not for us to count the number on her list or to shame a woman for having many lovers, but to applaud a person who—decades before women publicly stood up for their sexual and identity rights—was unabashed about her sex life. When I think about how liberated Frida was with her body, her marriage to Diego complicates the matter quite a bit. I'd like to praise her affairs, but the truth is that many of them occurred while she was married, and even accounting for her husband's infidelities doesn't change the fact that they were indeed in a marriage.

Vows aside, in Frida we get to know a woman who, long before the 1960s sexual revolution that made waves in the United States and beyond, was perfectly content not merely to explore her sexuality, but to be open about it. She did not apologize about her need for pleasure, just as she did not apologize if that pleasure was indulged with a man or a woman. No one could tell Frida Kahlo what to do with her body. And the same goes for the rest of us. For any of us struggling to embrace our sexuality or feel comfortable in our skin—no matter our gender or the gender of our partners—Frida would likely tell us some simple advice: "Make love, take a bath, make love again."

LOVE—OR LUST—LETTERS

Of course we know of Frida Kahlo's talent with a paintbrush, but the artist's diaries, letters, and poems reveal the way she had with words—particularly when it came to matters of the heart . . . and um, other parts. Here, an excerpt from a letter found in her diary offers a glimpse at how Frida lyrically described making love with her husband:

> *It was the thirst of many years restrained in our body. Chained words which we could not say except on the lips of dreams. Everything was surrounded by the green miracle of the landscape of your body. Upon your form, the lashes of the flowers responded to my touch, the murmur of streams. There was all manner of fruits in the juice of your lips, the blood of the pomegranate, the horizon of the mammee and the purified pineapple. I pressed you against my breast and the prodigy of your form penetrated all my blood through the tips of my fingers. Smell of oak essence, memories of walnut, green breath of ash tree. Horizon and landscapes, I traced them with a kiss. Oblivion of words will form the exact language for understanding the glances of our closed eyes. You are here, intangible and you are all the universe which I shape into the space of my room. Your absence springs trembling in the ticking of the clock, in the pulse of light; you breathe through the mirror. From you to my hands, I caress your entire body, and I am with you for a minute and I am with myself for a moment. And my blood is the miracle which runs in the vessels of the air from my heart to yours.*
>
> *The green miracle of the landscape of my body becomes in you the whole of nature. I fly through it to caress the rounded hills with my fingertips, my hands sink into the shadowy valleys in an urge to possess and I'm enveloped in the embrace of gentle branches, green and cool. I penetrate the sex of the whole earth, her heat chars me and*

my entire body is rubbed by the freshness of the tender leaves. Their dew is the sweat of an ever-new lover.

It's not love, or tenderness, or affection, it's life itself, my life, that I found [when] I saw it in your hands, in your mouth and in your breasts. I have the taste of almonds from your lips in my mouth. Our worlds have never gone outside. Only one mountain can know the core of another mountain.

Your presence floats for a moment or two as if wrapping my whole being in an anxious wait for the morning. I notice that I'm with you. At that instant still full of sensations, my hands are sunk in oranges, and my body feels surrounded by your arms.

THE SECRET BATHROOM

After Frida Kahlo's death, in 1954, Diego and the museographer and poet Carlos Pellicer transformed her beloved La Casa Azul into a museum honoring her life and work. As the two curated the house into an exhibition, they put anything they didn't consider relevant to Frida's legacy as an artist in the bathroom . . . and locked the door. That included her personal items—clothing, cosmetics, medicines, corsets, and a chest of drawers and trunks full of photos and letters.

Diego entrusted his close friend Dolores Olmedo with the keys to the bathroom, asking that it not be opened until at least fifteen years after his death. Dolores honored his wishes—and went well beyond them; the door wasn't opened until after her own death, in 2004. The museum's director, Hilda Trujillo Soto, says that Dolores was less concerned about keeping Frida's personal items hidden than she was about protecting the reputation of her dear friend Diego. In addition to clothing and cosmetics, behind the door that was locked for more than fifty years lay a trove of insight into Frida's life, including intimate descriptions of her affairs with her lovers Isamu Noguchi, Leon Trotsky, and more—information that the infamously possessive Diego probably wouldn't have tolerated being made public during his lifetime.

What Would Frida Do . . . if She Wanted to Seduce Someone?

An adjective often used to describe Frida is *seductive*. Despite the disabilities of her body, her less than traditional looks, and the pain of her past, she lit up any room and held an allure that was magnetic to both men and women. So how would *she* do it?

Own the room. Frida was known for being the center of attention, often eclipsing her more famous husband by spontaneously busting into song, telling hilarious stories, and offering up lewd jokes—to the delight of her guests, male and female.

Get poetic. Frida's diary and love letters show that she had a way with words. They illustrate that sex meant more to her than just a tryst or physical encounter—it was poetry. In today's world of sexting and social media direct messages, love letters might seem old-fashioned, but taking a cue from Frida's diaries could be exactly what you need to spice things up.

Have fun. Above all, even in matters of the bedroom, Frida's lust for life was apparent. Consider the number of lovers she took during her lifetime—and the stories told about her. Tales abound of a cheeky Frida holding interviews with reporters from her bed and never hesitating to open up about the details of her sex life with her husband . . . or her lovers.

8

IDENTITY

As our culture progresses toward celebrating what makes people different, Frida Kahlo's story only becomes more and more legendary, the tale of a woman whose actions made her a feminist, activist, and leader for gay rights way ahead of her time. Though she never called herself a feminist, and the word is much more popular now than it was during her lifetime, she never let her status as a woman stop her from anything—particularly from being shockingly candid in her work. But in her nearly five decades, of the many *-ist* labels she would have embraced, she would most likely have welcomed those of communist and Mexicanist.

Not a day went by in Frida Kahlo's adult life when she didn't wear her pride in her Mexican identity quite literally on her sleeve. From her paintings inspired by

Mexican *votos* (small, traditional religious paintings) to her Tehuana-inspired outfits to the decor in La Casa Azul, much of Frida's life and work was fueled by her appreciation for pre-Columbian Aztec and Mayan cultures and a dedication to her mother's indigenous mestiza roots.

Walking through La Casa Azul—now known as the Frida Kahlo Museum and set up exactly as Frida had it while she was alive—I was struck by how many details pay homage to Frida and Diego's country. In the entryway, an Aztec-style fireplace made of volcanic stone welcomes visitors. The kitchen's yellow, blue, and white color scheme feels instantly transporting; tiny brown-clay dinnerware on the wall spells out "Frida y Diego"; instead of a modern stove, Frida's kitchen holds a more traditional wood stove. In the dining room, the floor is painted yellow; blue and yellow dishes and glassware artfully line the cabinets; Mexican knickknacks and talismans sit on the shelves. Outside, the patio is a peaceful refuge overflowing with greenery; between blossoming flowers and trees stands a pyramid featuring Diego's favorite pre-Columbian idols.

Contrary to popular belief, it was not Diego who turned Frida's attention to Mexicanism *or* politics—but it *was* her marriage to Diego that solidified her fervent passion for representing where she came from. Aside from the practicality of wearing long skirts to hide her disabled leg, Diego encouraged his wife to wear Mexican-inspired fashions—and for both of them, her look wasn't just about style or aesthetics; it was a political statement.

Frida grew up middle class, in the quiet neighborhood of Coyoacán; there, *huapil* tunics and indigenous dresses were the attire of the working class. In fact, the emerald-green dress and red rebozo Frida donned on her wedding day

THE MOST IMPORTANT THING FOR EVERYONE IN GRINGOLANDIA IS TO HAVE AMBITION AND BECOME 'SOMEBODY,' AND FRANKLY, I DON'T HAVE THE LEAST AMBITION TO BECOME ANYBODY.

were borrowed from her maid, who was much more likely to wear such clothing than a member of the Kahlo family. By wearing styles more typical of the indigenous people of her ancestry—and purchasing them from Mexican artisans—Frida both supported and made a statement for *la raza.*

The artist's allegiance to her beloved Mexico was most apparent when she left it. In letters to friends and lovers during her travels to San Francisco, Detroit, New York, Paris, and elsewhere, a melancholy Frida often wrote about her homesickness for her country. She particularly disliked "Gringolandia," and she captured her longing for her homeland poignantly in her 1933 painting *My Dress Hangs There.*

She also made her need to return to Mexico known to her husband, who was not ready to head back given the success and fame he received in America. Eventually he gave in, but he didn't hide his resentment toward Frida. Publicly, he blamed the move on a lack of creative inspiration, but privately he made it clear to his wife that returning to Mexico was not what *he* wanted.

In time, though, Diego joined Frida again in a joint dedication to Mexico, and in the early 1940s, the pair began working on a project together: a temple they called Anahuacalli, built in the Pedregal district near Coyoacán. The structure was meant to be part home, part museum dedicated to Diego's collection of pre-Columbian idols, as well as a getaway from their "bourgeois" life in Mexico City. It became more of Diego's passion project, though Frida was always supportive. In her essay "Portrait of Diego," Frida called the site (which had, at that point, essentially become an archaeological museum), "sober and elegant, strong and refined, ancient and perennial; from its entrails of volcanic rock it cries out with voices of centuries and days: Mexico is alive!" The museum also inspired another of Frida's well-known works, *Roots,* which depicts Kahlo anchored to the Mexican earth by the stalks of a plant sprouting from her torso.

Frida's odes to Mexico increasingly emerged at the forefront of her work, particularly in two paintings from 1938. In *My Nurse and I,* which Frida considered one of her best paintings, a baby Frida with an adult head drinks the milk from her wet nurse's breast, offering the idea that Frida was fortified by her indigenous ancestry. (Frida's own mestiza mother, Matilde, could not breastfeed Frida because she was pregnant with Frida's sister, who was only eleven months her junior.) In the painting, Frida's nurse's face is covered by a black Columbian funerary mask because, Frida admitted, she could not remember what her nurse looked like. But the expression on the mask and the way the nurse holds the young Frida is almost sacrificial, and the blank expression on Frida's face shows an emotional disconnection from the nurse—who may possibly also represent her mother, with whom Frida had a complicated relationship.

The second painting, *Four Inhabitants of Mexico,* also features a young Frida, this time as a toddler sucking her thumb while sitting amid four symbolic characters with different ties to the country: a Judas, a pre-Columbian symbol from Nayarit, a Day of the Dead skeleton, and a straw man riding a donkey. Frida gifted the small painting to the actress Dolores del Río, telling her that the child in the photo wasn't actually her, but a representation of the child she could never have with Diego.

Frida's pride in her Mexican roots and her distaste for all things bourgeois—or, really, anything non-Mexican, despite the fact that her father was German—made it only natural that she would be inclined toward politics. But her

**MY PAINTINGS ARE . . .
THE MOST FRANK EXPRESSION
OF MYSELF, WITHOUT
TAKING INTO CONSIDERATION
EITHER JUDGEMENTS OR
PREJUDICES OF ANYONE.**

interest began long before she was Diego Rivera's wife, and even before she was an artist. As one of the few female students in Mexico City's National Preparatory School, Frida was outspoken about her socialist and Marxist-Leninist views, joining the Young Communist League and the Mexican Communist Party.

Throughout the rest of her life, she was in and out of the Communist Party (the outs often because of quarrels or disagreements her husband had with members of the party) and publicly supported the Mexican Revolution. She was particularly vocal about rights for workers, land reform in Mexico, and the Spanish Revolution of 1936. Her homes with Diego—both the bridged house in San Angel and La Casa Azul—became hubs for intellectuals and revolutionaries from around the world, who would discuss the issues of the day over meals whipped up by Frida's cook in her decidedly Mexicanista kitchen.

Frida's interest in politics and identity was perhaps more authentically motivated than Diego's; her attention-loving husband seemed mostly focused on how politics could help raise his status through networking and posturing. Frida, meanwhile, although passionate about politics, didn't like the *act* of politicking or networking, preferring to discuss her views on her own terms rather than engaging in forced conversations. In Hayden Herrera's biography of Frida, Jacqueline Breton remembers a trip the Bretons, Riveras, and Trotskys took together. During the getaway, Diego and the revolutionary Trotsky spent much time in the living room discussing politics—but Frida, who was vocal about her dislike of organized discussions instead of naturally occurring ones, opted instead to play games with Breton and sneak cigarettes outside.

Frida was strongly influenced by her husband's views and positions as a party leader, never hesitating to help by organizing rallies, writing Diego's correspondence, or even supporting his friend (and, briefly, her lover) Leon Trotsky when he sought asylum in Mexico City in the 1930s. But she was only vocal about what *she* felt strongly about. In 1936, for instance, she actively helped refugees from Spain who were escaping the Spanish Civil War, working with Diego to raise money for those seeking asylum in Mexico. (This included Ricardo Arias Viñas, who three years later became her lover.) She was staunchly outspoken and never afraid to take a stand, despite the fact that doing so, even in defense of her husband, was quite rare for a woman—particularly a Mexican woman—at the time.

In 1933, after Diego was fired from painting a mural commissioned by Nelson Rockefeller because of its overtly communist imagery, Frida attended protests decked out in her signature Mexican outfits—and refused to speak to Rockefeller when he approached her at an event. In a pre-internet world, to make her opinion known, Frida had no choice but to turn to the press, publicly calling out the Rockefellers by telling a newspaper, "The Rockefellers knew quite well the murals were to depict the revolutionary point of view—that they were going to be revolutionary paintings. They seemed very nice and understanding about it and always very interested, especially Mrs. Rockefeller. We were their guests at dinner two or three times, and we discussed the revolutionary movement at great length."

Years later when Diego got into a disagreement with the Riveras' friend Trotsky—who stayed at La Casa Azul for two years during his asylum—Frida took Diego's side, despite the fact that Leon was not just her friend but also her

I MUST STRUGGLE
WITH ALL MY STRENGTH
TO CONTRIBUTE THE
FEW POSITIVE THINGS
MY HEALTH ALLOWS TO
THE REVOLUTION, THE ONLY
REAL REASON TO LIVE.

ex-lover. She wrote to her friends Ella and Bertram Wolfe that "Diego has now fought" with the International Fourth (the global communist group led by Trotsky) and that he told Trotsky "to go to hell in a very serious manner. . . . Diego is completely right."

But when her former lover was stabbed to death with an ice pick to the skull by the anticommunist Ramón Mercader, it was Frida—then extremely ill—who was arrested and questioned about any potential involvement in the plot to assassinate him. The Riveras' feud with Trotsky was widely known, and the fact that Frida had been introduced to Mercader by mutual friends during her time in Paris, where Mercader was working as an undercover agent, and had had dinner with him made her a prime suspect. During twelve hours of interrogation, the police found nothing, and Frida was let go.

As Frida grew increasingly ill toward the end of her life, she was often in and out of the hospital for various procedures, after which she was prescribed bed rest at home. Her political passions helped to keep her occupied. She once wrote, "I must struggle with all my strength to contribute the few positive things my health allows to the Revolution, the only real reason to live."

On July 2, 1954, less than two weeks before she died, Frida was at her husband's side in a wheelchair to protest a coup d'état by the United States in Guatemala. (Looking to end the Guatemalan revolution and President Jacobo Árbenz's support of communists, the CIA wanted to install as president the military officer Carlos Castillo Armas—who would be the first of several US-backed dictators in the country.) Despite her doctor's orders to remain on bed rest after a case of pneumonia, Frida took to the streets.

Frida died eleven days later, on July 13, of a pulmonary embolism. After her death, a public procession accompanied her body to the cremation ceremony, during which a student draped a Mexican Communist Party flag over her coffin. The story goes that Diego would not let anyone remove it. As her body was cremated, family and friends sang traditional Mexican songs, including her favorite, "Cielito Lindo." Even after her soul left the world, Frida made her mark as an artist, a Mexican woman, and a revolutionary—a legacy that still, decades later, continues.

Considering Frida's work in its entirety, one thing is clear: her art would have been both less unique and less meaningful were it not for Frida's convictions. Some of her most familiar pieces are ruminations on communism or Marxism, and her pride in her Mexican identity is present in every one of her creations. Throughout her being, she was fiercely proud to be Mexican, just as she was to be a woman, to be sexually liberated, and to have her own political opinions.

Frida teaches us not only that is it okay to embrace our viewpoints, even if they go against the grain or the norm, but also that the celebration of our differences is what makes us special. If someone had questioned Frida's beliefs, she wouldn't have conformed to fit in—just as she never subscribed to anyone else's idea of what her art should look like, or what stories it should tell. Through her paintings, her protests, and her points of view, Frida sends a strong message: don't just *be* yourself—be loud and proud about it.

WHY MEXICO WAS ALWAYS HOME FOR FRIDA KAHLO

Diego's career and later Frida's own led her around the world; she lived in various cities, including San Francisco, Detroit, New York, and Paris. In each one, Frida frequently wrote letters professing her homesickness for Mexico—and famously, she didn't hold back about her feelings for the United States or Europe. Here, a snapshot:

IN A LETTER TO HER FRIEND AND MEDICAL ADVISOR DR. ELOESSER:

You might tell me that you can also live there without little cocktails and without "parties," but without them one never amounts to anything, and it is irritating that the most important thing for everyone in Gringolandia is to have ambition, to succeed in becoming "somebody," and frankly I no longer have even the least ambition to be anybody, I despise the conceit and being the "gran caca" does not interest me in any way.

IN A LETTER FROM PARIS TO HER LOVER, PHOTOGRAPHER NICKOLAS MURAY:

You have no idea the kind of bitches these people are. They make me vomit. They are so damn "intellectual" and rotten that I can't stand them any more. It is really too much for my character. I rather sit on the floor in the market of Toluca and sell tortillas, than to have any thing to do with these "artistic" bitches of Paris. They sit for hours on the "cafes" warming their precious behinds, and talk without stopping about "culture" "art" "revolution" and so on and so forth, thinking themselves the gods of the world, dreaming the most fantastic nonsenses, and poisoning the air with theories and theories that never come true. Next morning—they don't have any thing to eat in their houses because none of them work and they live as parasites off the bunch of rich bitches who admire their "genius" of "artists." Shit and only shit is what they are. I never seen Diego or you wasting their time on stupid gossip and "intellectual" discussions. That is why you are real men and not lousy "artists."—Gee weez! It was worthwhile to come here only to see why Europe is rotting, why all this people—good for nothing—are the cause of all the Hitlers and Mussolinis. I bet you my life I will hate this place and its people as long as I live. There is something so false and unreal about them that they drive me nuts.

A TIMELINE OF FRIDA'S POLITICAL PURSUITS

1922

Frida joins Los Cachuchas, a radical group at the National Preparatory School in Mexico City that passionately debated the views of revolutionaries like Vladimir Lenin and Karl Marx. The students were also known for playing pranks on their teachers. Many claim that long before Frida met Diego as an adult, she played pranks on him while he painted a mural at her school.

1924

Frida becomes an active member of the Mexican Communist Party's youth group.

1928

Despite the fact that it was publicly outlawed, Frida officially joins the Mexican Communist Party not long after being portrayed in one of Diego's murals handing out weapons while wearing a red shirt emblazoned with the party's sickle and hammer.

1929

Diego is expelled from the party for supporting the Soviet Communist Party's Left Opposition—and Frida follows his exit. That same year, Frida paints *The Bus*, a work that reflects on the class differences in Mexico—and in which her husband Diego's artistic influence can be seen. It depicts a housewife with a grocery basket, a working-class man in overalls, an indigenous mother breast-feeding her baby, a businessman holding a bag of money, and an adolescent girl with a red rebozo blowing in the wind.

1932

After several years spent living in the United States as her husband worked on various commissioned projects, Frida's disillusionment with "Gringolandia" and her connection to Mexico only deepen, as is apparent in her painting *Self-Portrait Along the Border Line Between Mexico and the United States*, which features an uncharacteristically demure Frida standing between the two countries while holding a Mexican flag, a statement of her allegiance to her country and distaste for the elitism of the United States.

1936

Frida, along with other socialist organizers, founds a committee to raise funds for Spanish Republicans fighting against fascism. Frida's role was to aid refugees in finding places to stay and to help them secure employment.

1937

With the Riveras' help, Russian revolutionary Leon Trotsky and his wife seek asylum in Mexico City—and stay for two years at La Casa Azul. After a falling out between Diego and Trotsky, the couple moves out, and the Riveras distance themselves from Trotskyism. In 1940, Trotsky is assassinated.

1948

Though Diego is rejected, the Communist Party accepts Frida's application to reenter the party.

1950

Despite being relegated to a bed at Mexico City's English Hospital, Frida remains as politically active as possible, inviting visitors to sign a petition to support the communist-led World Peace Council.

1954

Eleven days before her death, bound to a wheelchair but holding a banner reading "Por La Paz," Frida participates in a protest against US intervention in Guatemala. She joins more than ten thousand people in the streets of Mexico City to denounce the CIA-led coup against Guatemala's democratically elected president, Jacobo Árbenz, who the United States had decided was a communist and therefore must go.

A week and a half later, Frida's body was carried to her cremation ceremony, her coffin draped with a Mexican Communist Party flag.

What Would Frida Do . . . if She Wanted to Take a Stand?

Know your role. Throughout Frida's life, her husband was the face of the various movements they supported while she arranged things behind the scenes by writing letters, drafting speeches, and organizing rallies. She was fine with that; Frida never needed fame or notoriety, because she was motivated purely by her views. It's likely that without her passion in the background, Diego would have been less successful as a party leader and activist.

And your roots. Much of Frida's political point of view was shaped by her *Mexicanidad*, her love for her country, and her early upbringing during the Mexican Revolution. As an adult, she even changed her birth year from 1907 to 1910 to align with the start of the Mexican Revolution, denouncing colonialism and calling herself "a daughter of the revolution." Her personal communist agenda was greatly shaped by the classism and poverty she witnessed in her home country, and it was her pride for Mexico—which only grew thanks to her travels around the world with Diego and, later, to promote her own work—that influenced much of her work.

Find a partner with similar interests. It's true that Frida Kahlo had her own political stances before she met Diego Rivera, but their parallel views are a large part of what brought them together. Throughout their marriage (and even after their divorce) they were stronger politically as a dynamic duo; Frida wanted to support her husband because she knew that his work as a revolutionary made him happy, and Diego admired Frida for her outspokenness and candor. If one of them was invited to a political meeting, the other was often included, with requests for "Comrade Frida" to be present with her larger-than-life husband. When it came to changing the world, the two brought out the best in each other.

9

FRIENDSHIP

When we think about Frida Kahlo's relationships, we usually think about her marriage to Diego Rivera, or her several infamous extramarital liaisons (many of which were, yes, with members of the same sex). But Frida's diaries and her many letters show that her friendships were just as important to her as her romantic affairs. In today's era of "squad goals," it's important to remember that behind the strong, empowered artist was a group of people who lifted her up when she was down, stayed by her sickbed, and advised her on her illnesses, her art, and her roller-coaster marriage.

In return, Frida's gifts to her *queridos* included homemade meals in the kitchen of La Casa Azul (often prepared by her cook—Frida was admittedly not much of a cook herself, though her meals were offered with love and lots of tequila); portraits, her friends' likenesses frozen in time for millions of people around the world to admire; and long, enchanting letters filled with lyrical observations, precise attention to detail, and intricate, witty doodles.

In fact, it's because of those letters to friends—often signed with her lipstick print and "thousands of kisses"—that we know as much as we do about Frida's life outside her art.

Surprisingly, one of Frida Kahlo's first boyfriends—and the cause of her earliest heartbreak—became a dear lifelong friend. Alejandro Gómez Arias was the high school beau who was with Frida when she suffered the bus accident that affected her health for the rest of her life; he broke up with Frida as she was healing from her injuries. We can see from her letters that the teenage Frida was initially filled with resentment and angst at his decision to leave. During her convalescence in 1926, at age eighteen, as a gift to him she painted her first self-portrait—a romantic, Renaissance-style depiction of her in a red velvet gown—hoping it would lure him back to her. The painting would later become known as her first of many, but it only reconciled the couple temporarily before they broke up for good.

Eventually—even though she was married to Diego Rivera—Frida and Alejandro became close again, swapping letters through the years, with Frida addressing him as "Alex" and updating him on everything from her travels in the United States to the first European exhibition of her work in Paris in 1938. She wrote, "On the very same day as my exhibition, I want to talk to you even if just a little. Everything worked out perfectly and I have been ridiculously lucky. The crowd here is very fond of me and they are all extremely kind."

I CARRY YOU

WITH ME INSIDE,

ALWAYS.

Apparently, shortly after their breakup, Frida painted a portrait of Alejandro, but she didn't share the work with him until 1952, just two years before her death. She inscribed it, "Alex, I lovingly painted your portrait, which is a picture of my friend for all time. Frieda Kahlo. 1952. 30 years later." The art world only became aware of the painting in 1994, when relatives of Alejandro found the work in his home.

Another friend who was integral to Frida's story was the famed Italian photographer and activist Tina Modotti, known for her politically motivated snapshots of the working class. Modotti played two important roles in Frida's life. First, Diego and Frida were formally introduced to each other at one of Tina's parties in 1928. Second, Tina was active in the Communist Party, and she brought Frida into her circle of Marxists, artists, and avant-garde thinkers.

The fact that Tina was one of Diego's ex-lovers didn't stop Frida from befriending her, even though Modotti was reportedly the reason Diego and his second wife, Lupe Marín, parted ways. Tina's nude modeling for Diego turned into a yearlong affair. (It's said that Diego was the one who introduced Tina to communist ideals.) Still, Frida and Tina became fast friends and close confidants until Tina's death at age forty-five due to congenital heart failure. Rumor has it that the two might have been lovers, though no concrete evidence supports the story.

Befriending (and, yes, sometimes bedding) her husband's exes became a common occurrence in Frida's life. She even became friends with Lupe, whom Diego was married to (but allegedly separated from) when he met and began courting Frida, and who was the mother of two of Diego's children, daughters Guadalupe and Ruth. At first, Lupe pretended that her husband's relationship with Frida didn't bother her; she seemed amused when she described her first encounter with "the so-called youngster" and expressed her surprise that the twenty-one-year-old Frida "drank tequila like a real mariachi." But as a guest at their wedding, she reportedly drank so much that she could no longer mask her real feelings. By all accounts, Lupe made quite the scene, screaming at her ex-husband and comparing her legs to Frida's disabled one. Frida was so hurt that she stormed out of her own wedding reception.

Soon, Frida found herself swallowing her pride to ask Lupe for a little help. Apparently, her new husband could not stop raving about his ex-wife's cooking. Frida turned to Diego's *previous* wife for guidance, both on how to make his favorite meals and on how to withstand his incessant infidelity, which resumed almost immediately after Frida married him.

Frida and Lupe spent many long afternoons together, with Lupe teaching Frida her recipes and Frida venting about her increasingly complicated marriage. Frida sometimes painted as they chatted; in 1929, months after her wedding, she created a portrait of Lupe, and Lupe and her daughters remained important fixtures in Frida and Diego's lives until Frida's death.

The friend whose opinion Frida regarded the highest was Dr. Leo Eloesser. In 1930, when Frida Kahlo was brand new to the United States, living in San Francisco while Diego worked on a fresco for the stock exchange there, the chronic pain in her right foot forced her to seek medical care. Diego took her to see Eloesser, a graduate of Stanford's medical school and a renowned thoracic and orthopedic surgeon. After their first appointment, Dr. Eloesser became Frida's most trusted medical advisor, offering a fresh perspective on the

I WISH TO BE WORTHY,
WITH MY PAINTINGS,
OF THE PEOPLE
TO WHOM I BELONG
AND TO THE IDEAS
WHICH STRENGTHEN ME.

many years of contradictory diagnoses she'd received of her various ailments, the most problematic being the chronic foot pain. Once, when Frida lacked the money to pay him, she painted a portrait of him as a show of gratitude.

Their professional relationship naturally led to a friendship, and through years of Frida's physical and emotional challenges—and particularly throughout her relationship with Diego—Dr. Eloesser became a confidant and guide. When she and Diego were living in Detroit in 1932, Frida found herself pregnant against all the medical odds. She desperately reached out to Dr. Eloesser about how to proceed.

"Do you think it would be more dangerous to abort than to have a child?" she wrote.

> *If, on the contrary, you think having the child might improve my condition, then, in that case, I'd like you to tell me if it would be preferable for me to go to Mexico in August and have the baby there in the company of my mother and sisters, or whether it might be best to wait for it to be born here. . . . Doctorcito, you have no idea how embarrassed I am to bother you with these questions, but I see you not so much as my doctor as my best friend, and your opinion would help me more than you know.*

In her notes—usually addressed "Querido Doctorcito," or "Dear Little Doctor"—she asked for his general wisdom, addressing him more as a friend than as a professional. Although on the surface the two didn't have much in common, it's clear from their years-long conversation that the doctor's gentle demeanor, fluency in Spanish, and left-leaning views aligned with Frida's personality. The doctor even weighed in on her romantic affairs; he was largely responsible for the Riveras' reconciliation following their divorce in the late 1930s. After Diego visited Dr. Eloesser to inquire about the rumors of his ex-wife's declining health, the doctor wrote:

> *Diego loves you very much, and you love him. It is also the case, and you know it better than I, that besides you, he has two great loves—1) Painting 2) Women in general. He has never been, nor ever will be monogamous, something that is imbecile and anti-biological. Reflect, Frida, on this basis. What do you want to do? If you think that you could accept the facts the way they are, could live with him under these conditions, and in order to live more or less peacefully could submerge your natural jealousy in a fervor of work, painting, working as a school teacher, whatever it might be . . . and absorb yourself until you go to bed each night exhausted by work [then marry him]. One or the other. Reflect, dear Frida, and decide.*

Decide she did, because after her friend's letter, she headed to San Francisco to seek the doctor's treatment for her latest flare-up—where her ex-husband just so happened to be waiting for her. Soon thereafter, Frida painted another portrait dedicated to the *doctorcito* as a thank-you for his guidance: a depiction of herself wearing a necklace of thorns and the hand-shaped earrings gifted to her by Pablo Picasso when she was in Paris. In the painting, she looks both glamorous and desolate, a crown of vibrant flowers contrasting with the muted color palette of the background—possibly a reflection of how she felt when she was separated from Diego. The inscription at the bottom reads, "Doctor Leo Eloesser, my physician, my best friend. With all my love."

Another pair of friends who served as intermediaries for Frida and Diego were the Wolfes. Bertram Wolfe was a scholar and writer who, along with his wife, Ella, helped found the Communist Party USA. The Wolfes met the Riveras when they lived in Mexico City, and the four became lifelong friends. The two couples' habit of traveling together became difficult for Frida as her marriage grew rockier. Still, she never asked the Wolfes to choose sides. In 1934 Frida wrote to the couple—whom she lovingly called "Ella and Boit"—honestly and emotionally about her husband's affair with her sister Cristina: "You will neither take Diego's side nor mine, but rather simply understand why I have suffered *so much*, and if you have a moment free you'll write me, won't you? Your letters will be an immense consolation and I'll feel less alone than I am."

Many of Frida's letters and photographs have been released to the public courtesy of the Wolfes. Bertram was the author of the first extensive English-language biography of his friend Diego—titled *Diego Rivera: His Life and Times*—one of several he wrote about political activists including Vladimir Lenin, Joseph Stalin, and Leon Trotsky. In conducting research, he amassed a large collection of the Riveras' personal items.

For many years, the woman who had a front-row seat to the life of Frida Kahlo was Lucienne Bloch, a Swiss-born artist—and daughter of composer Ernest Bloch—whom Frida met at a banquet given by one of Diego's patrons in New York City in 1931. But Lucienne and Frida didn't immediately hit it off.

"I was sitting next to Diego," Lucienne remembered, according to Hayden Herrera's biography of Frida. "I took him over and talked and talked with him. I was very impressed with Diego's idea that machines were marvelous; all the artists I knew thought machines were terrible. Once in awhile I saw this Frida Rivera with her one eyebrow that crossed her forehead and her beautiful jewelry, just giving me these dirty looks." But Frida went even further: "After dinner, Frida came over to me, and she looked at me with a really sharp look and said, 'I hate you!' I was very impressed. This was my first contact with Frida, and I loved her for it. At the dinner, she thought that I was flirting with Diego."

Lucienne soon began work as Diego's art assistant, and she earned some notoriety as the only person to capture photographs of the infamous mural Diego painted on commission for Rockefeller Plaza, *Man at the Crossroads.* After protests about the murals' nods to communism, Nelson Rockefeller ordered Diego to stop painting, and the mural was removed.

Frida soon warmed to Lucienne, and they became close friends. In 1932, when Frida learned that her mother was dying, Lucienne—who was living with the couple in Detroit while Diego worked on his mural project—traveled with Frida via train from Michigan to Mexico City and back again. Earlier that year, she had helped Frida heal after her miscarriage, and she worked with Diego to rent a lithography studio for Frida to use. Using the method of applying ink to stone to print images on paper, Frida created *Frida and the Abortion* with Lucienne's assistance.

In a letter dated February 14, 1938, from Frida to Lucienne, who had recently shared the news that she was expecting her first child, we get a sense of the type of friend Frida was to her closest *amigas*:

> *Yes, Kid, you don't have any bad foot, but you are going to have a baby and you are still working, and that is really*

**WITH FRIENDSHIP
AND AFFECTION COMING
FROM MY HEART,
I AM PLEASED TO
INVITE YOU TO
MY HUMBLE EXHIBITION.**

> *swell for a young kid like you. . . . You don't know how happy I am with such news. . . . But please, do not forget that I must be the godmother of that baby because, in first place, it will be born the very same month that I came to this damn world, and in second place, I will be damn switched if somebody else would have more right than I to be your "comadre" so keep that in mind.*

Frida indeed became godmother to baby George, whom she enjoyed spoiling. She also spoiled her *amigas*, showering them with love and affection and never hesitating to let them know how important they were in her complicated story.

When we consider the lives of historic figures, we often focus on their significant others. But Frida is proof that we are only as strong as the people we surround ourselves with. Yes, Diego was an important piece of her narrative. But thanks to the hundreds of letters and diaries she left behind, we can see that when Frida was at both her highest and her lowest, it was her friends that she leaned on for venting, guidance . . . and sometimes, just a little bit of fun.

Like Frida, no matter how resilient we are, we can use a firm foundation to shore us up, whether it's via group chats or in gatherings with tequila. And we may have different friends for different needs. Dr. Eloesser was Frida's sage adviser on matters of life and health. Her sister Cristina was the one person who was always present by Frida's side—and despite the affair Cristina had with her sister's husband, their bond was unbreakable. Other friends encouraged her art and creative ambitions. If it weren't for Frida Kahlo's inner circle, she might not have become the icon we so admire.

Looking at how Frida's small but mighty crew supported her, we can think about our own supporters. We can ask ourselves: Who is *your* Dr. Eloesser? Your Cristina or Lucienne? No matter who we are—even if we have the strength Frida had—not a single one of us can make it through this thing called life alone. Even the darkest moments can be made brighter when we surround ourselves with people who have our backs.

THANK YOU FOR BEING A FRIEND

One of Frida's favorite ways to show her friends her appreciation and gratitude was by painting portraits of them. Here are a few:

***Portrait of Alicia Galant*, 1927:** Frida's early works were heavily influenced by the Italian Renaissance, as is apparent in this piece, which captures a high school friend posing aristocratically while wearing dark, sensual colors.

***Portrait of Lupe Marín*, 1929:** Just months after her wedding to Diego, a lonely Frida swallowed her pride and befriended Diego's ex-wife, of whom she soon painted a portrait. But their friendship had its ups and downs. You can only view this painting via a black and white photo, because Lupe reportedly tore it up with scissors after the two had an argument.

***Portrait of Alejandro Gómez Arias*, 1929:** Frida captured her high school sweetheart turned friend a few years after their breakup, but she didn't give the work to him until nearly three decades later, just two years before her death.

***Portrait of Eva Frederick*, 1931:** While many art historians believe that the subject of this portrait was simply a stranger Frida met while living in San Francisco, others claim that the Black model was either a friend or a romantic interest who posed for the artist—including for a nude pencil sketch that never made it onto canvas.

***Portrait of Dr. Leo Eloesser*, 1931:** The artist captured her beloved friend and doctor's "birdlike neck" and penchant for "high collars" in this painting. He is shown posing next to a model sailboat, an homage to his love for his own boat, which he sailed in the San Francisco Bay.

***Portrait of Natasha Gelman*, 1943:** Natasha was an immigrant from Czechoslovakia who, along with her husband, Jacques, had a particular interest in Mexican art. The Gelmans became close friends of the Riveras, and after Natasha passed in 1998, the Gelman collection became known for having many works by Diego and Frida.

***Portrait of Mariana Morillo Safa*, 1944:** Frida's portrait of a young, wide-eyed girl wearing a bow depicts the daughter of Frida's friend Eduardo Morillo Safa, an agrarian engineer. The Safa family remained close friends of Frida until her death. She also painted several other portraits commissioned by Eduardo, including one of him and his wife, Alicia. And she dedicated her self-portrait *Tree of Hope, Remain Strong* to Eduardo after writing to him about a botched operation she underwent in New York that left her with scars that "those surgeon sons of bitches landed me with." The painting features a dressed-up Frida next to another version of herself on a hospital bed, her back covered in bloody gashes; the phrase "Tree of Hope, Remain Strong" (a line borrowed from her favorite song, "Cielito Lindo") is written in Spanish on a flag she holds.

***Self-Portrait with Portrait of Doctor Farill*, 1951:** Frida's last signed self-portrait depicts her in a wheelchair painting the likeness of her surgeon, Doctor Juan Farill, who had performed seven surgeries on Frida in the previous year. She clasps a palette that, instead of paint, appears to hold her heart—a sign that Frida created this work with all her heart as a gift for the doctor who worked hard to help her heal.

FRIDA AND CRISTINA

Frida's longest-lasting and closest friendship was always with her younger sister, Cristina—whom she affectionately called *la chapparita*, or "shorty." In the last decade of her life, Frida wrote in her diary about her childhood, recalling memories from as far back as kindergarten, when she and Cristina were sent to the same class together despite their age difference. It's clear from Frida's recollections that the two were inseparable; one of Frida's earliest portraits, painted in 1928, was of her sister.

After Cristina's affair with Diego, Frida was able to forgive Cristina first before her husband; Cristina later proved her loyalty to her sister by covering for her or offering her home as a getaway for Frida's secret rendezvous with various lovers. Frida was also particularly close with Cristina's two children, Isolda and Antonio, whom she spoiled with gifts and by paying their school tuition; both would later say that they essentially grew up at their aunt Frida's house.

In Hayden Herrera's biography *Frida*, the author cites multiple sources who recalled that before any surgery, Frida would refuse to be anesthetized unless Cristina was present to hold her hand. Her sister often invited guests to Frida's hospital room to enjoy her homemade enchiladas and moles—and, of course, tequila—as they kept the patient entertained. During the last year of Frida's life, Cristina rarely left her sister's side. Even after the most unforgivable betrayal, in Cristina and Frida Kahlo's case, the old adage that blood is thicker than water was indeed true.

What Would Frida Do . . . if She Wanted to Build a Strong Inner Circle?

Host gatherings. No matter where they lived around the world, and despite their marital troubles, Frida and Diego were known for hosting memorable parties and making their home feel like *everyone's* home. Both the San Angel house and, later, La Casa Azul became the main meeting places for friends of the Riveras, who would come over to enjoy conversation, tequila, and Oaxacan-style mole.

Incorporate mutual friends with your significant other. Frida and Diego's social lives were intertwined; even during their brief divorce, they were known simply as "Frida and Diego." Yes, double dates and parties at the Riveras' were common, but the couple also made many mutual friends—and neither seemed to force their acquaintances to choose sides when they experienced relationship woes.

Give personalized, thoughtful gifts. Frida's gifts were usually in the form of portraits; she depicted her loved ones on canvas through her own eyes, capturing their likenesses forever. Of course, when she painted many of these works, she had no idea of the worth they would one day hold for their owners. Her personalized touches didn't just end with paintings for her friends; she also sent letters filled with quirky doodles and funny cartoons, sealed with a kiss using her own lipstick.

10

VIVA LA VIDA

In almost every piece of work I've read reflecting on the life of Frida Kahlo, one word appears again and again to describe what the artist embodied: *alegría*. The literal translation from Spanish means joy or happiness, but it's also used to describe a state of being—a lust for life. And that is something Frida Kahlo never lacked, despite a rough start to her life, a rocky marriage, and years of illnesses. In pop culture today, she's often portrayed as a dark, serious artist and revolutionary, but by all accounts, the real-life Frida was hilarious—silly and even childlike, full of pranks, jokes, and laughter. And even when life threw the worst kinds of challenges her way, Frida Kahlo found the humor and beauty in those dim moments.

While writing this book, I've learned a lot about what it means to live life to the fullest. Whenever I feel tired after a long day of work, or complain about this friend or that family member, I imagine Frida appearing to interject her opinions. By now, I feel that she and I are well acquainted, and I've gotten to know her proclivity for over-the-top stories flourished with dramatics, almost always ending with a dose of black humor.

When I type late into the night, her presence is often by my side as I write about her years spent imprisoned within corsets and other contraptions, about the heartbreak of her infertility, and about the loneliness of it all. With each word, my own grievances feel small, like insignificant minutiae. This fictional Frida doesn't hesitate to hop in and out of my life to put things into perspective—to show me that with a little *alegría*, truly nothing in this life can be *that* terrible.

No story better illustrates the real Frida's lust for life than the entrance she made to her final art exhibition. In April 1953, Mexican photographer Lola Alvarez Bravo sensed that the end was near for her friend Frida who, after undergoing a bone transplant, was deteriorating fast. Lola organized an exhibition at the Galeria Arte Contemporaneo in Mexico City, which would be the first-ever solo show of Frida's work in her home country. At the time, the artist was confined to bed, barely able to stand on her own for more than ten minutes. Still, the idea of displaying her work for her friends and the people of Mexico apparently gave her a boost of energy. From bed, she put all her efforts toward helping to plan the event, even handcrafting invitations tied together with ribbons and featuring a poem written in her own hand. Here's the verse in English (though it's worth noting that in Spanish, it delightfully rhymes):

I AM NOT SICK.
I AM BROKEN.
BUT I AM HAPPY
TO BE ALIVE AS LONG
AS I CAN PAINT.

With friendship and affection born from
the heart, I have the pleasure
of inviting you to my humble
exhibition.
At 8 in the evening—you have a watch,
after all—I'll wait for you in the
gallery of that Lola Alvarez Bravo.
It's located at Amberes 12 and with doors
open onto the street, so don't get
lost because that's all I'm going to
say.
All I want is for you to tell me your
good and sincere opinion: you are
well-read and well-written, your
knowledge is first-class.
These paintings I painted with my own
hands and they wait on the walls to
please my brothers and sisters.
Well, my dear cuate *[friend], with true*
friendship I thank you with all
my heart.

—Frida Kahlo de Rivera

Unfortunately, even with all the excitement, Frida's health worsened to the point that her doctors forbade her from leaving bed, much less attending an exhibition, even her own. So Frida thought of a clever way to make sure she could be there for her debut while following the doctor's orders: she had her bed delivered to the exhibition so she could attend *from* bed.

Minutes after the doors opened to a packed crowd (newspapers and onlookers would later report that the line to enter had wrapped around the street corner), Frida arrived via ambulance on a hospital stretcher, dolled up in her standard Mexican-style dress and costume jewelry. She was deposited onto her bed, where she lay for the remainder of the show. The crowd queued up, eager to catch glimpses of or greet Frida, who was tired yet jovial; attendees remembered her holding court like a queen, drinking and singing Mexican *corridos* with her guests. She was as much a work of art as the paintings that surrounded her.

It was an entrance that has gone down in the history books, the moment that officially launched Frida's star . . . just a little over a year before her death. Her work from the exhibition garnered interest from patrons around the world, located as far away as Paris and New York. For Frida, the celebration was bittersweet. In his 1960 autobiography, Diego would recall of his wife's big night, "I thought afterwards that she must have realized she was bidding goodbye to life."

Frida would hold on to that life for fifteen more months. The following August, after years of surgeries, the removal of multiple toes, and, finally, a lingering bout of gangrene, Frida's doctors decided to amputate her leg. During this period, Frida's alegría began to fade, if only temporarily. As an invalid, she dealt with physical pain while also mourning the loss of her leg. She sketched haunting drawings in her diary of herself as a one-legged doll, or showing her face crying beneath the moon as her body disintegrated into the ground. On one page, she sketched her feet standing on a pedestal, detached from her body, with the caption "Pies para que los quiero si tengo alas pa volar?" ("What do I need feet for if I have wings to fly?")

Even after having her leg removed and spending every day trapped in bed with nothing but her journal-writing and her painting, Frida placed one passion above all else: Diego, *el niño de sus ojos*, the child of her eyes. A diary entry shows where her worries truly lay: "It is certain that they are going to amputate my right leg. I know few details, but the opinions are very serious. . . . I am very worried, but at the same time, I feel that it will be a liberation. I hope I will be able, when I am walking, to give all the strength that I have left to Diego. Everything for Diego."

One woman can only be so strong, and after her surgery Frida became weaker and weaker, on both the outside and the inside. Frida's nurse, Judith Ferreto, believes that Frida tried to take her own life, a suggestion that is affirmed by Frida's diary entries from this dark time, including a poem she wrote with the lines: "YOU ARE KILLING YOURSELF / There are those who *will no longer forget you* / I accepted its strong hand / *Here I am*, so that they should live."

As the artist hung on, her husband was often at her side. At first, as he wrote in his autobiography, it was a struggle: "Following the loss of her leg . . . Frida became deeply depressed. She no longer even wanted to hear me tell her of my love affairs, which she had enjoyed hearing about after our remarriage. She had lost her will to live."

Diego was dedicated to keeping his wife's spirits up, spending time by her bedside telling stories and singing her favorite songs. Three months after her amputation, Frida learned to walk using a prosthetic leg, and her reclaimed independence seemed to bring back some of that alegría. The 2019 traveling exhibition *Appearances Can Be Deceiving* featured

NOTHING IS ABSOLUTE.
EVERYTHING CHANGES,
EVERYTHING MOVES,
EVERYTHING REVOLVES,
EVERYTHING FLIES
AND GOES AWAY.

many pieces from Frida's wardrobe. One standout was a pair of Chinese-style red leather boots she had specially made after her amputation, which have small dangling bells and gold trim. It was in those shoes that Frida began not just to walk but to dance again.

At this point, Frida was often in a drug-induced state, and the pain, her frustrations, and the medications apparently left her in a foul, angry mood. She was prone to tantrums triggered by her lack of control over her body and the increasing distance from her "child" Diego. Her diary reflects her state of mind, with pages upon pages of bleak, often incoherent ramblings paired with drawings depicting her physical struggles. Here and there, however, you detect glimpses of the old, joyful Frida. In an entry from February 1954, she wrote, "I have achieved a lot. I will be able to walk, I will be able to paint, I love Diego more than I love myself. My will is great. My will remains."

Yet Frida and Diego's marriage was still stormy. Diego seemed to be caught in a push-pull between wanting to be there for his wife and being unable to bear witness to her suffering. According to writer Raquel Tibol, Diego said at the time, "If I were brave, I would kill her. I cannot stand to see her suffer." The discomfort of seeing his beloved in pain led Diego to spend more and more time away from Frida's side, which only worsened her suffering. "No one knows how much I love Diego. But neither does anyone know how difficult it is to live with that señor," she wrote. "And he is so strange in his way of living that I have to guess whether he loves me; because I think that he does love me, even if it is 'in his way.' I always say this sentence when our marriage is discussed: that we have joined 'hunger with the desire to eat.'"

With a little help from the drugs (and the cognac she consumed to relieve her pain), Frida did some painting in the final months of her life; many of her last works were still lifes that managed to be simple while also infused with splashes of euphoria. But she was also present enough to make several paintings that contained political statements. *Self-Portrait with Stalin* features the artist seated in front of a painting of the communist revolutionary. The more intricate *Marxism Will Give Health to the Sick* portrays an angelic Frida in a corset as giant hands from a saint-like Karl Marx reach down as though to "save" her; her crutches are tossed to the side, and a peaceful dove hovers behind her.

According to Hayden Herrera's 1983 biography of Frida, in June 1954, a month before her death, Frida's condition began to improve slightly, and as her mood became more jovial, she also grew more hopeful, making plans to travel, adopt a child, and celebrate her twenty-fifth wedding anniversary with Diego (clearly ignoring that short divorce), which would happen in August. In advance of their milestone, Frida had purchased an antique gold ring as a gift for her husband and began telling friends they should prepare for a grand "Mexican fiesta."

All her plans were thwarted when, in typical Frida fashion, she ignored her doctor's orders to stay in bed as she recovered from pneumonia. Instead, she headed out in a wheelchair pushed by Diego to a communist demonstration protesting the United States' move to oust Guatemala's liberalist president Jacobo Árbenz. A photo from the event is often shared on the internet to show Frida the revolutionary—but because the image is usually presented out of context, it's shocking to realize that the determined woman holding a poster reading "Por La Paz" was less than two weeks away from her death. Perhaps the only sign in the photo of Frida's fading joie de vivre is her face, which, upon closer inspection, appears exhausted and aged beyond her years.

The outing caused Frida's pneumonia to worsen, and she knew it. The final pages of the diary she kept for the last decade of her life feature dancing skeletons dressed up in costumes and scribbled musings like "We look for calm or 'peace' because we anticipate death, since we die every moment." On July 6, she celebrated her 47th and final birthday and was carried down to the kitchen of La Casa Azul to be surrounded by friends, mole, tamales, and tequila.

The final entry in Frida Kahlo's diary features a green-winged angel with blackened legs flying upward into a colorful sky. Her last written words became some of her most iconic, the words of a woman who was both morbid and reflective yet full of—there's that word again—alegría. "Espero alegre la salida y espero no volver jamás," she wrote. "I hope the exit is joyful—and I hope never to return."

Frida Kahlo died on July 13, 1954. The official cause was a pulmonary embolism. There has been much speculation that, having reached the end of her ability to bear unthinkable pain, Frida might have taken her own life with a drug overdose; according to her nurses and doctors, it wouldn't have been the first time she'd tried. Still, both the medical reports and Diego's account specify that an embolism was the true cause.

"I sat beside her bed until 2:30 in the morning," Diego wrote in his autobiography. "At four o'clock she complained of severe discomfort. When a doctor arrived at daybreak, he found that she had died a short time before of an embolism of the lungs. When I went into her room to look at her, her face was tranquil and seemed more beautiful than ever."

She had seemed to know how near the end was. He wrote, "The night before she had given me a ring she had bought me as a gift for our twenty-fifth anniversary, still seventeen days away. I asked her why she was presenting it so early and she replied, 'Because I feel I am going to leave you very soon.'"

Even so, Diego believed she had fight left in her: "But though she knew she would die, she must have put up a struggle for life. Otherwise why should death have obliged to surprise her by stealing away her breath while she was asleep?"

After her death, the Riveras' friends ensured that she was celebrated with the same zest she embodied while alive. They dressed her in a black Tehuana dress with her signature costume jewelry and braided her hair with ribbons and flowers just as she had worn it while she was alive. Her bed was surrounded by her favorite dolls and pre-Columbian idols. Dozens of visitors came to visit Frida for one last time before she was cremated, per her wishes.

As for Diego? Onlookers say the death of his wife instantly aged him, and that he looked as though his soul were "cut in two." A day after her death, he asked a doctor to cut Frida's skin open to make sure she didn't bleed—that she was *truly* dead, because he simply could not believe it.

Frida was transported to her memorial service in a coffin from the National Institute of Fine Arts, with honor guards that included former president Lázaro Cárdenas. As loved ones carried her, a student threw a bright red flag emblazoned with the communist symbol of a hammer and sickle onto her casket. Though some in Frida's circle wondered if they should remove it, at Diego's request the flag remained, a final nod to Frida's status as a revolutionary.

Photographs show hundreds of mourners following Frida's casket as it was carried to the crematorium; inside, she lay with her head surrounded by red carnations, her shoulders covered in her favorite rebozo. During the procession, friends and luminaries including writer Andres Iduarte and poet Carlos Pellicer read eulogies and sonnets. At Diego's request, as Frida's body entered the crematorium, her loved ones sang her favorite songs, including the mariachi classic "La Llorona" and ballads like "Adios, Mariquita Linda."

A tale has been passed down from onlookers at Frida's cremation who reported a strange occurrence—perhaps one last Frida-style joke from the afterlife. After her corpse entered the burning oven, the intense heat from the blaze caused her lifeless body to sit up straight. As Frida's hair caught fire, it created a halo around her face, and she appeared to be wearing a smile.

I had always assumed that Frida's final resting place was somewhere near her parents' or ancestors' burial sites. So I was surprised when I visited Museo Frida Kahlo—formerly La Casa Azul—to notice a small, toad-shaped clay urn in her bedroom. There was no sign, no "Here Lies Frida Kahlo." In fact, I might have missed the urn entirely if not for the audio guide I'd purchased at the front desk that pointed it out. Frida's ashes are displayed simply, without fuss, in the room where she spent many hours writhing in pain, singing with friends, and painting the portraits that built her legacy. There Frida Kahlo rests, overlooking her beloved garden.

Just like that, the life of an artist, lover, wife, friend, and revolutionary came to an end in the middle of the night—but her legacy had only just begun. Even the Frida who gritted her teeth through the pain to make her way to her first Mexican solo exhibition on an ambulance stretcher,

I HOPE THE
EXIT IS JOYFUL—
AND I HOPE
NEVER TO RETURN.

greeting hundreds of fans, couldn't have envisioned that someday, more than sixty years in the future, she would be a household name around the globe. I can't imagine that she ever had an inkling that she would become an icon who would appear in hundreds of exhibits, movies, plays, and books—like this one. And she also probably had no clue that the life she lived so courageously would inspire countless people to emulate even a small bit of her fearlessness.

What would Frida do if she needed a reminder to live life to the fullest? She would be grateful for every moment of every day—down to the tiniest detail, whether it was carefully planning her outfit or taking extra care as she set the table for a meal. She would love without hesitation or abandon, pour her passion into her work, her politics, her friends, and her significant other—even when the world told her *not* to. And she would tell her story in her own way, viewing her tales through her own brilliant lens, writing them down, painting them.

I think Frida left her simplest but most important piece of advice for us in one of her final works. Days before she died, Frida got out of bed to walk over to a still life of sliced watermelons she had painted the previous year. It was an ode to the fruit often presented to the dead as part of Mexico's Día de los Muertos holiday. It would be the last work that she signed her name to—and on the flesh of the melon, she wrote, "Viva la Vida!"

As I write these words, my imagined Frida smiles at me, satisfied that I've finally gotten it. "It's really not that complicated after all," she tells me. "Just live your damn life, *cuate*—every second of it."

FRIDA'S FAVORITES

Frida's passions included art, tequila, and of course, Diego. But what else did she love?

FOOD

In America, according to Herrera:

Frida had no use for the bland American cuisine, though she finally developed a taste for three native concoctions: malted milk, applesauce, and American cheese. She ate quantities of hard candies or sticky sweets like taffy and nougat that reminded her of cajeta, the caramelized goat's milk from Mexico. Even after she discovered several small grocery stores that catered to the Mexican population of Detroit, and managed to cook Mexican meals, the electric stove she was forced to use seemed to her perversely intractable.

She once wrote from New York to her friend Isabel Campos in Mexico, "As soon as I arrive you must make me a banquet of pulque and quesadillas made of squash blossoms, because just thinking about it makes my mouth water. Don't think I'm forcing this on you and that already from here I am begging you to give me a banquet. It's just that I am reminding you, so that you don't look wide-eyed when I arrive."

MUSIC

Frida was as devoted to Mexican music as she was to Mexican culture, but she had eclectic taste. Growing up, she listened to her father play Beethoven and Strauss on the piano, which inspired an interest in classical music, and as an adult she was a fan of and befriended composers, including George Gershwin. During a visit to La Casa Azul, I was surprised to see that among her belongings were many jazz records by artists such as Duke Ellington. But it was indeed music from her culture that she treasured the most; during gatherings at La Casa Azul, Frida loved to play traditional folk songs and classics like "Cielito Lindo" and her lover Chavela Vargas's version of "La Llorona." A line from the former, "Arbol de la esperanza, mantente firme," inspired her painting *Tree of Hope, Stay Strong.*

BOOKS

Frida's home, now the Museo Frida Kahlo in Coyoacán, has several floor-to-ceiling shelves that are packed with books. I was surprised by the fact that in the various descriptions of Frida's likes and loves, books are never mentioned, yet her home overflowed with tomes ranging from travel guides (covering China, Italy, Brazil, and more) to medical and botanical books, poetry anthologies, crime thrillers, and novels. Many of her books had flowers pressed between their pages. Her copy of Walt Whitman's *Leaves of Grass* was found full of dried petals and leaves; it was displayed at London's 2018 Victoria and Albert Museum exhibition with the pressed flowers intact.

FRIDA ON THE BIG SCREEN

Frida Kahlo loved going to the movies, but she often skipped the latest artsy releases being discussed in her inner circles in favor of lower-brow offerings like *Godzilla*. While Diego worked—especially in the early days of their marriage—she spent afternoons either with friends or solo sitting in the darkness of a theater, enjoying a film. Her own remarkable story has been depicted many times onstage and on screen, including:

Frida Kahlo and Tina Modotti **(1982):** As interest in the lives and works of the two female artists experienced a resurgence during the women's rights and other movements of the 1970s and 1980s, this documentary explored the pair's friendship, their art, and their individual impacts on feminism.

Frida Still Life **(1983):** Mexican director Paul Leduc released this drama about the artist's life starring Ofelia Medina as Frida. The movie won several awards and was praised for being an example of New Latin American cinema. For nearly two decades, it was the only well-known film about the life of Frida.

Frida **(1991):** This opera about her life premiered at the American Music Theater Festival in Philadelphia, a successful show that was reprised two years later—and then again in Guadalajara, Mexico, in 2007, with a Spanish translation to celebrate what would have been Frida's one hundredth birthday.

Frida **(2002):** The best-known movie about the Mexican artist was released after years of speculation regarding a major Hollywood adaptation of Frida's story. Early names attached to the project included Madonna, but Salma Hayek ended up portraying Frida in the whimsical Julie Taymor–directed film, which earned Oscars for Best Original Score and Best Makeup, plus a Best Actress nomination for Hayek.

***The Life and Times of Frida Kahlo* (2005):** This ninety-minute documentary produced by PBS and narrated by actress Rita Moreno explored the artist's life, work, and impact on art and politics.

***Coco* (2017):** Pixar's animated ode to Mexico's Día de Los Muertos—and to the importance of remembering our ancestors—features a memorable cameo from Frida Kahlo. She appears in the afterlife to help the film's protagonist, Miguel, sneak into a concert where she's performing. Even as a Disney character, Frida wears her signature Tehuana-inspired look, complete with a floral headdress—and a spirit monkey, of course.

Love Is in the Details

For Frida, there was magic even in the tiniest of moments. Throughout her life, friends and acquaintances took notice of the care Frida put into every aspect of her day. In the mornings or before any outing, she took hours to pull together her outfits and hairstyles, wandering her garden to choose the perfect flowers to weave through her braided hair, and matching her ribbons and costume jewelry to her dresses just so. Meals took a long time for Frida to prepare as she contemplated how to arrange dishes she'd spent the day shopping for at a local market, surrounding them with fruit and flowers as though she were composing a still-life painting. She was an artist by trade, but for Frida Kahlo, life was her canvas.

ACKNOWLEDGMENTS

This book is dedicated to Frida, but it was also written in loving memory of my grandmother, Granny, who took me to bookstores on the weekends during my childhood and never complained when I stopped paying attention because my nose was in a book.

Mom and Dad: Thank you for all the love, support, and sacrifices that led to the opportunities that made it possible for me to achievc my dream as a writer. Those "Hooked on Phonics" lessons really paid off for your *hija* and Puddy! I love you. To my sissy Amaiya: Whether I'm forgetting what to pack in my suitcase or am spiraling about deadlines—as I did many times with this book—thank you for always being the calm in my storm. I am blessed to have a sista girl as wise and loving as you. To my favorite boys, Demetrius, Logan, and Parker: I love you guys! To my grandmother Tata: Long before I understood who Frida was, it was you who showed me what a strong Latina looks like. Titi: As soon as this book hits the stands, I'm taking you up on one of those "spoiling your niece" days. To my godmother, Eve, my godfather, Uncle Rick, and all of the Cuzin-Sista-Friends and families: I'm blessed to have grown up surrounded by such an incredible extended family. To the Funn-Diaz clan: You all inspire me, and even though you left us for the West Coast, I miss you more than you know.

Now for my crew, who I could always count on no matter what for support, laughter, or margaritas throughout the creation of this book. Justine: We've had each other's backs since we were babies in the bathtub, and that will never change, even now that I'm a published author and you're a nurse saving the world. To my bestie Serena: Your nickname became Lightbright as a joke, but you have truly become the brightest light in my life, no matter how dark things get. My boo Joseph: What would I do without you? It means the world to me to know that no matter what, I always have your support—I'm so glad I have you in my life to push and inspire me. Devin: Thank you for always talking me off the ledge, pushing me to take the big opportunities, and for helping me feel ready for *What Would Frida Do?*

Stephanie King: I am blessed to have a friend like you who is so thoughtful, caring, and encouraging. So glad our friendship has blossomed over the years both as women and as writers; I can't wait for Ella Grace to read this someday! (And Lionel, too :) Steph and Manouska: Our group chat keeps me uplifted, even through ambitions like this book—as do our tequila dates.

And to Jay: I could not have written this book without you and your Jay Santana motivational talks. Thank you for being my cheerleader and for making me better, braver, and bolder; I love you. Or as Frida would say: I sky you.

To my OprahMag.com team: I am in awe of you guys every single day. Thank you for always inspiring me, and for encouraging me on this venture. To Gayle King: You were the best boss and are the best role model I could've ever asked for. Thank you teaching me to be not just a great journalist, but a great human. To Kate Lewis and the Hearst family: Writing this book felt even more perfect knowing I had your support. I'm proud to work for such an incredible company.

To my Penn State family, Uncle Ben, Dean Selden, Dean Hardin, and the College of Communications: I am the writer and journalist that I am today because of all of you. Thank you. And to my sorors of Alpha Kappa Alpha Sorority, Inc—particularly DG Sp '07, Divyne Awakening—the lessons this sisterhood and all of you have taught me and continue to teach me are endless.

To my agent, Wendy Sherman: It's been a delight to entrust this book to you; I knew from day one I was in good hands, and I'm looking forward to many more projects together. As for the Seal Press team at Hachette—to my editor, Emi Ikkanda: Your keen eye, whip-smart edits, and clear love of Frida made this book sing. Sharon Kunz, Jessica Breen, Allison Finkel, Abigail Mohr, Kait Howard, Katherine Hill, Kelley Blewster, and Kaitlin Carruthers-Busser—you all have shown me it really *does* take a village; I'm grateful to have worked with each of you in this process! And to Laura Mazer: Thank you for your vision—and for pushing me to answer the question what *would* Frida do?

Finally, to all the little Black and brown girls out there: Whether it's a canvas like Frida's, or a stage, or a manuscript—keep dreaming. As women, we're not often taught that it's okay to be ambitious, or to go after what we want. But the world is your oyster if you hustle hard and dream big enough. Don't ever take no for an answer—Frida wouldn't hear of it.

SOURCES

This book would not have been possible without the Frida Kahlo writers, experts, and researchers who came before me. It was a joy getting to know the life of Frida and referencing many works for this book, including:

Frida, by Hayden Herrera (Harper Collins, 2002 [1983]).

My Art, My Life, by Diego Rivera and Gladys March (Dover Publications, 1991 [1960]).

Frida by Frida: Selection of Letters and Texts, Foreword and Notes by Raquel Tibol (Editorial RM Mexico, 2003).

Frida Kahlo: Song of Herself, by Salomon Grimberg (Merrell Publishers, 2008).

The Diary of Frida Kahlo: An Intimate Self-Portrait, Introduction by Carlos Fuentes (Abrams, 2005).

And special thanks to Museo Frida Kahlo in Mexico City, which helps Frida's life and legacy continue every day.

© Oneika Raymond

Arianna Davis lives in New York City surrounded by way too many stacks of books. She is the digital director for *O, The Oprah Magazine* and previously worked at Refinery29 and *Us Weekly*. She has also written for *New York Magazine*, *Glamour*, *Marie Claire*, and PopSugar Latina and has served as an entertainment expert for Access Hollywood, Tamron Hall, VH1, TLC, and more. Follow her on Instagram at @ariannagab and Twitter at @ariannagdavis.